SECURE THE BAG!

Empowering Women and Building Wealth Through Smart Investing

C J Douglas

TABLE OF CONTENTS

INTRODUCTION

—◆—

Girlies,

The path to lasting financial independence is paved with knowledge and confidence. If there's one thing I've learned over the years, it's that you have the power to take charge of your financial destiny. Ignore for a moment, every lingering doubt you've had about your financial ability. Ignore the doubting voices that shut you down from time to time, making you wonder whether you have what it takes, because you do!

I'm writing this letter to you, a letter I wish someone would have written to me earlier on in my life. I'm imploring you to embrace the empowering world of investments. The journey might seem daunting at first, but remember, you have the strength and capability to navigate this successfully.

As you work your way through financial investments, you'll learn so much, not just about money, but also about yourself, and more importantly, how to conquer your fears around money.

I do understand that our curriculums have never really given much attention to personal financial management, a problem that has plagued society for years. Yet, this is one of the most important lessons in your financial journey. I'm talking about your mindset about money, your perception of loans, how you budget your income every month, your perspective on savings, and so on. These are crucial skills that go a long way in transforming your overall outlook of money, and in the long run, your pursuit of financial independence.

Start by learning about the fundamentals of financial investments. Dive into the world of stocks, bonds, and mutual funds, and grasp the concepts that shape the financial landscape. When it comes to money and investments, knowledge will always be your greatest ally, so don't shy away from learning the language of investments.

Embrace it with the same determination you bring to every aspect of your life.

As I write this book, I reminisce about the days when I had no knowledge of risk or my perception of it. I never realized that my perception of financial risk was intertwined with my perception of life, my beliefs, and my core values.

Understanding risk is crucial. Just as in life, there are uncertainties in the financial markets. Instead of fearing them, learn to manage and mitigate risks. Equip yourself with the tools to make informed decisions, and remember that every successful investor has faced challenges and uncertainties along the way. Embrace the learning curve, and let it be a testament to your resilience.

Don't hesitate to seek guidance. No one has ever made it on this journey alone. Engage financial experts, join investment groups, and participate in discussions. Collaborate with others who share your goals and learn from their experiences. Remember, financial empowerment is not a solo journey. Support each other, share insights, and collectively uplift one another on the road to financial independence.

Above all, trust in your abilities. Your foray into the world of financial investments may seem intricate, but remember, you are resilient, intelligent, and capable.

Rise up to the challenge, learn from every experience, and watch as your journey toward long-term financial independence unfolds.

You have the power to shape your financial destiny—seize it with confidence, and let your financial independence become a beacon of hope for others, and many generations to come.

Best,

C.J.

Secure the Bag!

Almost reads like a cliché, right? But it isn't.

In a world where so much is stacked against you, the one thing you need to win back is power and control over your finances. I wrote this book to empower you on your journey to financial independence, offering insights into money management, investing, and building wealth. I understand the diversity of beliefs surrounding financial matters, hence my intention to simplify investment concepts, making them accessible to women of all backgrounds and levels of financial literacy.

I encourage you to explore and define your personal financial philosophies, fully aware of the fact that individual perspectives shape how you approach spending, investing, and saving. I also encourage you to reflect on your values and beliefs, so you can make financial decisions that align with your unique goals.

For most women, the journey toward financial independence is often fraught with external pressure, particularly from family expectations and societal norms. We will discuss practical insights and strategies to help you navigate the complexities of financial autonomy. By addressing the unique pressures that women face this book serves as a guide to carving out your own path towards financial freedom.

A key concept you'll pick up throughout this book is the need to start early and start where you are today. This is how you tap into the power of compound growth and is a testament to the fact that even modest investments made early on can lead to substantial wealth over time. When it comes to investment, it's always wise to instill a sense of urgency—the motivation you need to take charge of your financial future. More importantly, remember that despite the occasional commonality of purpose, you are on your own journey, different from everyone else's. Do not allow yourself to be swallowed by the scourge of comparison. Instead, be confident in the knowledge that it's never too late to start investing for your long-term financial well-being.

The journey to financial empowerment means that you'll occasionally have to navigate biases that can cloud your decision-making. Common biases include fear of missing out (FOMO), overconfidence, herd mentality, and excessive risk aversion, which unknown to most people, can greatly influence your investment decisions. You can overcome this by becoming aware of the inherent biases and working around them to make smarter choices. This is how you cultivate a robust investment mindset that will always be resilient against common bottlenecks in the financial sector.

I'm fully aware of the fact that in some cases, investment can be daunting, and that's why a lot of people tend to avoid it altogether. To that end, this book breaks down intricate financial jargon, offering clear explanations and real-life examples. Through accessible language and relatable scenarios, you will gain a practical understanding of different investment principles, strengthening your confidence and ability to explore the world of finance.

I strategically planned the book into four parts, each serving as a building block for your financial journey. The structure ensures a natural progression starting with understanding basic financial philosophies and culminating in practical investment strategies that will shape your future. This gives you a comprehensive roadmap for sustainable financial empowerment and also ensures that the learning process is intuitive and impactful.

Ultimately, this is more than just a financial guide; it's a transformative journey that equips you with the knowledge and confidence to master your financial destiny. From digital platforms to modern investment strategies, my goal is to make sure that you are not only informed but also adept at navigating the complexities of dynamic financial investments.

Secure the Bag! stands as a true testament to the transformative power of financial literacy. By empowering you to overcome challenges, seize opportunities that come your way, and make informed financial decisions, together, we can cultivate a community of financially confident and independent women who blossom into a force for positive change in their lives and the lives of those around them.

PART I:

INVESTING 101

CHAPTER 1:

The Rich vs. the Wealthy: Which one Do You Want to Be?

—♦—

"Think about your future for a sec: Are you after riches or wealth?"

Now, that's a bit confusing, right? Most people use the terms rich and wealthy interchangeably, and therein lies the first problem we need to solve.

Secure the bag! Girl, get that bag! You've heard these phrases thrown around from time to time, but have you ever stopped to ask yourself what the end game is? More importantly, what's your endgame? I'll cut to the chase, being rich doesn't necessarily mean that you're wealthy, or financially stable for that matter. Being rich simply means you're a high-income earner.

With the kind of income you're bringing in, you should be able to afford a decent, comfortable lifestyle, luxury spending, and consumption here and there. The problem with being rich is that you are mostly focusing on the present and for that reason, it might not necessarily imply long-term financial stability.

Now, on the other hand, being wealthy is about so much more than being a high income earner. It's about acquiring and managing valuable assets, including properties, investments, or businesses, with the aim of steadily increasing your net worth over time. Wealth is more about accumulated resources, for example, real estate, investments, and businesses, which ultimately signify a broader and wholesome financial profile.

I know we all have different circumstances, and for that matter, you might be working hard to get from where you are to a point of financial stability. Well, if you can do all that, why stop there? Why not keep going until you become wealthy? There's a level of financial independence that comes from amassing wealth that changes not just your life, but could be the cornerstone on which you build and sustain generational wealth beyond your existence.

So, I'll not wait until the end of this chapter, or book for that matter, to answer the pertinent question, which one would you rather be; rich or wealthy? I'll choose wealth any day, and so should you.

One thing I'll advise you to do is change your mentality and approach this from a corporate perspective. Think about it for a moment. What's the one thing that every employer out there keeps thinking about in strategy meetings?—Sustainability! The emphasis is always on making sure that the business can ride out a difficult economic phase, weather the storm of new entrants into the market, outdo competitors, reinvent their marketing strategies, and so on. All these approaches are aimed towards making sure that the business remains a going concern (accounting assumption that the business meets all its financial obligations) in the foreseeable future.

So, what is the meaning of sustainability to you?

The idea is quite simple: create an investment plan that will ride out the difficult moments without you worrying about cashing out unnecessarily. This is a long-term plan, so you probably start by diligently allocating a portion of your monthly income toward your retirement account and taxable brokerage account. In your retirement account, you opt for low-cost index funds like the S&P 500, while in your taxable brokerage account, you carefully choose individual stocks of companies with strong growth potential. Aware of the higher risks associated with individual stock investments, you hold onto these for many years, understanding that consistent contributions and patience are key to achieving your financial goals.

Despite the fact that the market can be unpredictable, you must be steady in your approach. This means, periodically reviewing your portfolio to make sure your investments still match your long-term objectives. Over time, your disciplined strategy bears fruit, culminating in a substantial financial backup plan that gives you security and peace of mind as you approach retirement age. This is exactly how companies plan for sustainability, they think long-term.

That's the mentality I'd implore you to embrace as you read this book. If you're thinking about sustainability, you'll understand the difference between riches and wealth. More importantly, you'll understand the fact that you are capable of so much more than you might give yourself credit for. This is where you set your goals for the future, paving the way for the kind of investor you envision yourself to be, a moment of introspection that helps you realize where you are today, and what you must do to get to your desired financial destination.

Wealth is enduring. Wealth transcends your current sources of income, economic fluctuations, and any other bottlenecks that you might face. Wealth is long-term and generally comes with a strategic approach to financial management, including investment diversification and long-term planning. Wealth is empowering.

Who You Are as an Investor?

Wealth is empowering indeed. Imagine being able to accomplish everything you've often set aside because you didn't have the money. This brings us to an important question—what kind of investor are you? Now, for most women, this isn't an easy question to answer, especially if you barely grasp the fundamental concepts of investing. In my previous book, *Personal Finance for Teens & Young Adults: Life Skills Not Taught in the Classroom: Maximize Understanding of Banking Basics, Budgeting & Money Management* we explored the idea that this disconnect usually comes from the fact that none of this is taught in school, yet that's the one place we hope to learn most of the important lessons about life.

The school curriculum has its flaws, but that's all there is to it. You're at a point in life where you make different choices, and take responsibility for your actions. From here onwards, therefore, you choose to go the extra mile and pursue long-term financial success in ways that you never would have imagined.

One of the most important and personally revealing things every investor needs to do is to understand their motivations. Knowing yourself is the first step to building a successful investment profile. You might not realize this yet, but every investment decision you make is subconsciously informed by your beliefs, attitude, and past experiences. This is what makes up your investor personality.

Understanding oneself is quite a transformative journey with numerous benefits. It raises your awareness of your flaws, giving you a platform to build self-love and acceptance. With this confidence, you can comfortably navigate investments without worrying too much about external factors beyond your control.

Self-awareness is also an important component of emotional intelligence, a crucial investment skill most people overlook. It gives you insight into different perspectives and helps you understand how to set aside personal views and make rational decisions. A lot of people make investment losses not because they put their money in the wrong asset, but because they held on longer than they should have, usually for sentimental reasons.

Even though your investment approach might be about making money, there's got to be something bigger in it for you. When you think about your goals, try and categorize them into short-term and long-term objectives to create a balanced roadmap for your personal and professional life. What happens after you achieve your goals? What if you don't achieve them? There's always a lesson at every point of success or failure in investment. How you interpret these lessons will be greatly influenced by your core values. At the end of the day, you're working towards a sense of purpose and fulfillment, which you unlock along the way as you create your wealth through investment.

When I talk about beliefs, attitudes, and personal experiences, I'm alluding to the psychological aspect of investment. Your personality goes a long way in the kind of choices you make in the market. One important feature is risk tolerance. How comfortable are you with the prospect of loss? Are you the kind of investor who seeks the thrill of uncertainty, or are you drawn to investments that guarantee safety? Knowledge of your risk profile could give you more insight into your investor personality, and help you understand why you take the kind of risks you do.

Overall, it's important to understand the psychological aspect of investment to help you figure out the kind of investor you are. Here's a simple self-assessment test to help you understand your investor personality better.

Understanding Your Psychological Approach to Investing

Read each statement carefully and choose the response that most accurately reflects your feelings or behaviors in the context of investing.

Risk Tolerance

- I am comfortable with taking significant risks for the potential of high returns.
- I prefer moderate risks, balancing potential gains with potential losses.
- I am risk-averse and prioritize the preservation of my capital over potential gains.

Cognitive Bias

- I actively seek out information that aligns with my existing investment beliefs.
- I try to consider a variety of perspectives and information sources before making investment decisions.
- I often find myself sticking to my initial opinions and overlooking conflicting information.

Emotional Resilience

- I remain calm and focused on long-term goals during market fluctuations.
- I sometimes feel emotional during market downturns but try to stay focused on the bigger picture.
- Market volatility significantly affects my emotions, leading to impulsive decisions.

Decision Making

- I make investment decisions based on careful analysis and a well-thought-out strategy.
- I consider both rational analysis and gut feelings when making investment decisions.
- I often make impulsive decisions based on emotional reactions or short-term market trends.

Behavioral Finance Awareness

- I am familiar with concepts like herd behavior and loss aversion and actively consider them in my investment approach.
- I have a basic understanding of behavioral finance concepts but may not always apply them in my decisions.
- I am not familiar with behavioral finance concepts and their relevance to investing.

Results

The category with the highest count represents your dominant investor personality type.

If most of your answers checked the first box, you probably have an adventurous investor personality, are comfortable with high risks, and are open to seeking potential high returns.

If most of your answers checked the second box, you have a balanced investor personality, considering both rational analysis and emotions in your investment decisions.

If most of your answers checked the third box, you are a cautious, risk-averse investor who prioritizes capital preservation over potential gains.

Note that this guide is only a starting point to show you how to assess your investor personality, so it is not quite comprehensive. As you spend more time in the investment market and come across different investment opportunities, your assessment dynamics will keep evolving, so you can adjust the assessment metrics accordingly. Ideally, you should assess your risk appetite based on your personal and financial goals, and prevailing market conditions.

Who You Want to Be?

Given what you now know about the kind of investor you are, we circle back to the question we asked at the start of this chapter, what do you want to be? We already elaborated on the difference between being rich and wealthy, so your next challenge is how to use what you already know about your investor profile to make this happen. Are you happy with the results of your introspection? If not, what do you feel you should change in your investor profile so that you can become wealthy?

While investment takes place in the financial markets, the most important investment takes place in your mind. You have to win the psychological battle and rewire your brain to become the investor you wish to be. Here are some simple tips to help with this:

- Create time for personal reflection, to understand your risk tolerance, inherent cognitive biases, and your emotional state in different market conditions. Identify and acknowledge your investment strengths and weaknesses, embracing a realistic view of your abilities.
- Stay informed about behavioral finance concepts and psychological factors influencing your investment decisions.

Read books and articles on investor psychology to deepen your understanding of common biases and pitfalls.

- Cultivate mindfulness to become more aware of your emotional reactions during market changes. Evaluate your feelings before making investment decisions, ensuring they align with your long-term strategy.

- Actively seek out diverse perspectives and information, challenging your confirmation bias before making investment decisions. Consider opinions that differ from your own and explore a wide range of insights into your decision-making process.

- Gradually expose yourself to different levels of risk to assess your comfort zone. Set clear risk management strategies to protect your investments during market downturns.

- Always think long-term. Regularly review your long-term investment goals. Remember that short-term market fluctuations may not necessarily affect your overall financial objectives, so you'll mostly just have to be patient and ride them out.

- Finally, identify personal behavioral triggers that might result in impulsive decisions. Create strategies to mitigate these triggers, for example, setting clear rules for buying or selling investments.

Remember that in the long run, investment requires patience and discipline. Give your investments some time, and be disciplined in following your investment plan. Short-term market movements can trigger an impulsive reaction, so you must learn to be patient. Consistent self-awareness and proactive efforts to manage psychological biases will go a long way in helping you embrace the kind of mindset that helps you secure the bag!

The assessment above is important because it plays into your investment goals. The first step in every investment, especially for beginners, is to outline your goals and create a blueprint for your success. Let's explore four reasons why setting investment goals is important:

1. Goals give you a clear purpose. They help you understand why you are investing, or what you are working towards. Defining specific goals helps you articulate your financial objectives. Whether it's saving for a home, funding education, or building wealth for retirement, knowing your purpose provides direction and motivation.
2. Clear goals help you understand your level of risk tolerance. Note that different investment goals may require varying levels of risk. Assessing your risk tolerance early on allows you to align your investment strategy with your risk profile.
3. Goals help you establish an appropriate measure of success. This allows you to track progress and adjust your strategy accordingly.
4. This is also a yardstick for discipline and helps you stay focused. A well-defined plan reduces the likelihood of making impulsive decisions based on short-term market movements. Besides, once you understand your emotional connection to your goals, it gets easier to avoid impulsive decisions, a crucial feature for long-term investment success.

Investments can be frustrating at times, especially when the market seems to be swinging against you. When this happens, your goals provide the motivation and commitment to stay the course. They are your reminder of where you are, and what you are working towards. Knowing the purpose behind your actions reinforces a long-term commitment to achieving financial success.

Set Your Investment Goals in 10 Steps

Here's a simple 10-step guide to help you when setting investment goals. This worksheet gives you a comprehensive overview of your financial goals, risk tolerance, and a clear plan for achieving success in your investments.

- **Step 1: Define your financial objectives**—What are your primary financial objectives for investing? (e.g., buying a home, funding education, retirement)
- **Step 2: Assess your risk tolerance**—How comfortable are you with taking investment risks? (High, Medium, Low)
- **Step 3: Determine your time horizon**—When do you plan to achieve your financial goals? (Short-term, Medium-term, Long-term)
- **Step 4: Set specific and measurable goals**—What is the specific amount or target you aim to achieve for each financial goal? (for example, $50,000 for a down payment on a home)
- **Step 5: Align goals with your values and lifestyle**—How do your financial goals align with your values and lifestyle? (for example, travel, philanthropy, early retirement)
- **Step 6: Identify potential challenges**—What obstacles or challenges might you encounter on the path to achieving your goals? (for example, job loss, unexpected expenses)
- **Step 7: Evaluate your current financial position**—What are your current income, expenses, and savings? How much can you allocate towards your investment goals?
- **Step 8: Develop an asset allocation strategy**—What mix of assets (stocks, bonds, real estate) aligns with your risk tolerance and goals?

- **Step 9: Create a SMART action plan**—Break down your goals into Specific, Measurable, Achievable, Relevant, and Time-bound (SMART) actions. What must you do to achieve each goal?
- **Step 10: Monitor and adjust**—How often will you review your progress, and what criteria will you use to determine if adjustments are needed?

Now that you've done a complete investment assessment, let's build on this and explore the importance of investing in the next chapter. Remember, even though there are different reasons for investing, your decisions must always align with your personal and financial goals.

CHAPTER 2:

Why Invest? It's More Than Just a Gimmick

It's quite surprising that a lot of people hold onto the misconception that building wealth while you're young is merely a gimmick. From experience, the opposite is true. Investment is a smart way to build wealth, and the secret is to start as soon as possible. As the popular saying goes, the best time to plant a tree was 20 years ago, but the next best time is right now. Starting young is basically like giving your future self a high-five, and trust me, your future self will thank you for it.

Picture this: You're in your 20s or 30s, just starting out in adulting. Retirement might not seem like something you want to think about right now but guess what? Time is on your side, and that's your secret weapon in the investing game. Keeping some money in an investment account is like planting a money tree. Over time, it earns interest which also keeps earning interest, especially when you invest in an account that earns compound interest. It's like a financial snowball effect, and this is how you turn your modest contributions into a safety net when you retire.

The earlier you start, the more time your money has to work for you, thanks to the compounding interest effect. Now, I get it. The idea of retirement might seem a distant concept at the moment, but believe me, it sneaks up faster than you think. Starting early not only helps you ride out the market's ups and downs but also gives you the flexibility to take calculated risks. So, seize the moment! Even if it's just a small chunk of change, start investing now.

Saving vs. Trading vs. Investing: What's the Difference?

Let's dive into the dynamic trio of investing, savings, and trading. These three are the backbone of building and managing your wealth. Investing is like planting seeds for future benefits, savings act as your financial safety net, while trading is a thrilling roller coaster ride of short-term gains. Buckle up as we explore the dynamics of these three concepts, and help you understand their important role in your future.

Investment

When you're investing, you're essentially committing money or capital to an asset or venture with the hope that it will generate a return over time. The main goal of investing is to grow your wealth by taking advantage of compound returns, appreciation, and income. You're also hoping that the market will swing in your favor for the better part of the period you invest your money.

The difference between investing and the other two is that you typically have a longer-term perspective, often with the intention of holding onto the assets for an extended period, for example, a couple of years or even decades. There are different asset classes under which you can invest your money, for example, stocks, bonds, real estate, and mutual funds.

It's also important to note that all investments inherently carry some level of risk, and for that reason, your expected returns will depend on the prevailing market conditions and the performance of your chosen investments.

Investors typically conduct thorough research on potential assets, considering factors such as company fundamentals, market trends, and economic indicators. This due diligence informs your decision to buy and hold assets for an extended period.

Note that since investment decisions often involve a long-term perspective, it demands patience and discipline. You may use strategies like dollar-cost averaging, where you consistently invest a fixed amount over time to reduce the impact of market volatility.

Investments generally deliver higher returns over the long term. This is because the focus is on capital appreciation, dividend income, and compound returns. While there are risks, the historical trend has shown that well-managed investments tend to grow in value over time, providing a potentially substantial return on investment.

Saving

Saving is the process of setting aside money for future use or for emergencies. Savings are usually held in easily accessible and low-risk accounts, such as savings accounts or certificates of deposit (CDs). Most people use their savings accounts as a backup plan for short to medium-term needs, for example, setting up their emergency fund, making a down payment on a house, or covering random unexpected expenses without having to cash out from their investment accounts.

Savings accounts generally offer low-risk, stable options, but also provide lower returns compared to investment accounts. This is because the goal of saving is to preserve capital instead of seeking significant growth. Common savings options include your savings account, money market accounts, and other low-risk financial instruments.

The mechanics of savings involve regularly setting aside a portion of income into low-risk accounts that you can easily access. It's quite a straightforward process since all you are doing is amassing capital instead of being actively involved in the investment markets. Most savings decisions revolve around budgeting and planning for your financial goals. This is why savings come in handy for short-term projects.

A typical savings account carries low risk, hence the ability to offer more stability and security. Unfortunately, the returns are typically lower compared to investments. Since the primary goal is capital preservation, the returns may not always keep pace with inflation and the cost of living. Therefore, saving is more about having a financial safety net rather than achieving substantial growth. It is also advisable to seek savings products that can mitigate the risk of inflation outpacing your interest rate.

Trading

Trading refers to the act of buying and selling assets like stocks, bonds, currency, derivatives, or commodities. The main objective in trading is to profit from short-term price movements. For this reason, traders are mostly active in the markets they participate in, monitoring price movements to execute swift trades that capitalize on market fluctuations.

Traders generally operate on a short-term time frame, at times as brief as a few minutes, and in some cases, lasting a number of days. Given the short window of opportunity, trading can be considered a high-risk venture since you are betting on a careful assessment of price volatility in your desired market over a short period of time.

Trading is naturally a speculative venture, which also explains why it carries a higher level of risk than investing. That being said, the potential for quick gains is quite attractive and balances out the risk of rapid losses. Common examples of trading include swing trading and day trading.

To capitalize on short-term price fluctuations, traders generally use technical analysis, charts, and other tools to study the market and make immediate decisions. This also means the prospect of executing multiple trades within a single day.

Trading decisions are more frequent and reactive, requiring a keen understanding of market timing and trends. Beyond what you already know about the market, you might also have to research other strategies to help you exploit short-term price movement in the market.

Trading can offer quick, short-term gains, but it also comes with higher risks. The potential for significant returns is balanced by the possibility of instant loss. Timing precision is of utmost importance as a trader, because things change so fast, and success is never guaranteed in a trader's market.

Here's a summary of the three approaches:

Feature	Trading	Savings	Investment
Time Horizon	Short-term (minutes to days)	Short to medium-term	Long-term (years to decades)
Objective	Profit from price fluctuations	Capital preservation	Wealth growth and appreciation
Mechanics	Actively buying and selling	Regularly saving money	Research, strategic decision-making
Decision-Making	Reactive and frequent	Goal-oriented and consistent	Informed and patient
Risk Level	High	Low to moderate	Moderate to high
Returns	Potentially high, but risky	Low, stable	Potentially high, with long-term focus
Assets	Stocks, currencies, commodities	Savings accounts, CDs, low-risk investments	Stocks, bonds, mutual funds, real estate
Involvement	Actively monitors market trends	Minimal market monitoring	Periodic monitoring and adjustment
Commitment	Requires frequent attention	Limited involvement	Requires periodic review and adjustment
Goals	Capitalizing on short-term opportunities	Building financial safety net	Building long-term wealth

The Inflating Value of Being Alive

If you've been thinking about making your money work for you, you've probably looked at a number of investments already. But, have you ever stopped to wonder why you should invest? I mean, besides the fact that you want to put your money to work, is there more to it? Well, here are some reasons why investment is a brilliant idea, and more importantly, how your plan can help you outpace inflation.

- **Preserving your purchasing power**: Inflation erodes the purchasing power of your money over time. Any investment with the potential to generate returns above the inflation rate can help preserve and even increase the real value of your money. This is why it's always advisable to consider the cost of inflation when making investment decisions. Investing in real assets like real estate or commodities, for example, is a smart way to hedge against inflation. Since these assets appreciate in value over the long term, they can help you maintain your purchasing power.
- **Think about long-term wealth accumulation**: Your investments are an opportunity to harness the power of compounding, where earnings on your investments keep generating additional returns over time. This compounding effect is particularly potent when you hold on for the long term. This also makes your investments a crucial part of your retirement plan. By investing in assets that appreciate over time, you can accumulate sufficient funds to maintain a certain lifestyle once you retire.
- **Income generation**: Some investments, for example, stocks, pay regular dividends, which will provide a steady stream of income. To protect this income agenda, you need to diversify your investments and spread the risks accordingly. Each asset class responds differently to economic conditions, reducing your overall portfolio risk.

Inflation-Proofing Your Investments

Inflation is a persistent increase in the prices of goods and services over time, leading to a decline in the purchasing power of your money. Future-proofing your investments against inflation goes a long way in maintaining financial stability and ensuring that your wealth does not lose value over time. Here are a few real-world scenarios to illustrate the impact of inflation and how investments can help outpace it.

Let's say you plan to retire in 30 years. If the average inflation rate is 3% per year, the cost of living would double over that period. Without investments whose returns are higher than the rate of inflation, retirement savings may not be sufficient to maintain your desired lifestyle. By investing in growth assets like stocks your portfolio can grow over the long term, possibly faster than the rate of inflation, assuring you a comfortable retirement.

If you have kids, you are probably saving for their college education over the next 15 years. If education costs are rising at a rate higher than the general inflation rate, traditional savings methods may not work for you in the long run. Instead, you should consider investing in education-focused funds or other growth-oriented assets to keep up with the rising costs of education.

Real estate is often considered a hedge against inflation. Suppose you purchase a home as an investment. Over time, the property's value may appreciate in response to inflationary pressures in the housing market. If you are earning rental income from the property, this can provide a steady stream of cash flow, helping you offset the impact of inflation.

Apart from the real estate sector, you might also want to look at fixed-income investments, for example, bonds. The returns from such investments are usually guaranteed and made apparent at the point when you make the investment. If the interest earned on these investments is not higher than the rate of inflation, your real income will decrease over time. You can mitigate this by diversifying your investment portfolio with assets that have the potential for capital appreciation, for example, dividend-paying stocks. This goes a long way in mitigating the risk of inflation on your expected returns from fixed-income investments.

You can also look at this from the perspective of your everyday expenses, and purchase of goods and services. Look at your household budget for groceries, healthcare, and utilities. Over time, inflation pushes up the costs of these purchases. If you don't have investments that generate returns higher than the inflation rate, your household's purchasing power diminishes. To afford these necessities, you must invest in assets that have historically been proven to outpace inflation, like real estate.

By extension, if you are running a business, inflation makes it more expensive to run and manage your operations. You can work around this by strategically investing in efficiency improvements, better technology, and diversified supply chains to mitigate the impact on your profit margins.

It's clear that as a smart approach to investment, you must consider the impact of inflation; otherwise, it will eat into your profits, leaving you worse off, despite putting in considerable effort. Investments play a crucial role in mitigating the erosion of purchasing power caused by inflation. By strategically allocating assets, diversifying portfolios, and choosing investments that historically outpace inflation, individuals and businesses can build a resilient financial foundation for the future.

The Magic of Compound Interest

Simple interest and compound interest are two distinct methods for calculating the interest on a sum of money over a specified period. These approaches vary fundamentally in their treatment of interest accrual and its impact on your overall investment.

Simple Interest

Simple interest is a straightforward method. It calculates the interest on an initial principal amount over a set period. The formula for simple interest is **I=P×R×T**, where

- I represents the interest.

- P is the principal amount.
- R is the rate of interest per period.
- T denotes the time in periods.

The defining characteristic of simple interest is that it accrues solely on the original principal throughout the entire duration. There is no consideration for the interest earned in previous periods, resulting in a linear accumulation of interest over time. The total amount at the end of the period is obtained by adding the simple interest to the principal: **A=P+I.**

Compound Interest

In contrast, compound interest incorporates the effect of interest accumulation on both the principal and the previously earned interest. The compound interest formula, $P\ (1 + R/n)^{nt}$, takes into account the principal amount (P), the annual interest rate (R), the number of compounding periods per year (n), and the time in years (T).

In compound interest, the interest is compounded periodically, leading to exponential growth in your investment. The more frequent the compounding intervals, the greater the impact on your expected overall return.

The main difference between these two methods is that while simple interest is linear, and focused solely on the original principal, compound interest introduces the compounding factor, giving you a more dynamic and potentially lucrative method of interest accrual.

Compound interest can transform even modest savings into substantial wealth over time. The good thing about compound interest is the fact that it can generate earnings for you not only on the initial investment but also on the interests subsequently accumulated from previous investment periods. This compounding effect accelerates the growth of your money exponentially, creating a snowball effect that becomes increasingly powerful with each passing year.

Now, imagine tapping into this potential from a young age. Starting early on the journey of saving and investing grants you an unparalleled advantage in that the earlier you begin, the more time your money has to work for you. When it comes to investment, time is your greatest ally, allowing you to build a substantial financial foundation that can withstand the test of time.

We've delved into the captivating world of compound interest, unraveling its ability to exponentially grow your wealth over time. As we explore "The Easy Guide to Early and Smart Investments" in the next chapter, I implore you to build on the foundation of compound interest and get an early start to investment as actionable steps for your financial success.

Interactive Element

Let's say your investment goal is saving $1.5 million for future use. It could be for retirement, to buy a house, travel around the world, and so on. How much must you save each month to achieve this, and for how long?

As we mentioned in our discussions, the secret to a successful investment is to start as early as possible. I'll give you three possibilities, starting at the age of 20, 30, and 40. Suppose you are investing in an account that earns 7% interest—compounded every month—increasing your contributions every year by 10% to account for the cost of living adjustments like inflation, lifestyle changes, and so on.

If you start at 20, and save $500 a month, you will hit your $1.5 million target by the time you turn 48, with deposits of around $800,000. If you keep this up until you retire at 60, you will have saved well over $6.4 million.

If you start at 30, and save $1,000 a month, you will hit your $1.5 million target by the time you turn 52, with deposits of around $857,000. If you keep this up until you retire at 60, you will have saved well over $4.1 million.

If you start at 40, and save $2,000 a month, you will hit your $1.5 million target by the time you turn 57, with deposits of around $975,000. If you keep this up until you retire at 60, you will have saved well over $2.4 million.

The point of this exercise is to prove to you that it's always best to start investing as early as possible. This gives you more room to enjoy the power of compounding interest. If you start later in life but want to achieve the same goals, you'll have to save more every month, so essentially, you must work harder for your money to deliver the results you seek.

CHAPTER 3:

The Easy Guide to Early and Smart Investments

The prospect of financial freedom, wealth accumulation, and securing your future fuels your eagerness. You're ambitious, and determined, and maybe have a few tips from well-meaning friends or family members who've dipped their toes into the investment waters before you. Everyone's talking about investment, and the potential returns seem too good to pass up. But alas, you're also aware that the market can be a fickle beast at times, and there's always a chance that you could lose your investment.

So, how do you find the perfect balance between investing your money and being careful enough not to lose everything? This is a common question I get when I engage young women from time to time. Unfortunately, the business of investment has often seemed like a mysterious place to be, hence many people avoid it altogether. What you might not know is that this doesn't always have to be the case.

There are lots of young women who are making it big in the investment world, and all they had to do was start somewhere. You don't have to wait until you save a lot of money. You are not raising a downpayment for a house, you are dipping your feet into financial investments, and in the long run, you might even save enough to afford a downpayment on the house you want.

You can already tell where I'm going with this—you've got to start early. The earlier you start investing, the better prospects you can look forward to. Successful investment requires skill, discipline, and a level head—qualities that take time to cultivate. If you start today, you get a few more years of practical learning experience than if you start ten years from today. There's nothing as bad as making rookie mistakes in your portfolio at an advanced age in life.

For example, there's always the perennial risk of chasing hot tips and rumors, luring you into investments based on hearsay rather than thorough research. You hear whispers of a surefire stock poised to skyrocket or a revolutionary cryptocurrency bound for the moon. Without hesitation, you jump on the bandwagon, only to discover that the supposed golden ticket was nothing more than fool's gold. With your wallet lighter and your confidence shaken, you realize the importance of due diligence and critical thinking in the unpredictable world of investing. Such are common mistakes people make all the time, but you don't have to become another unfortunate statistic. In this chapter, we'll explore the easiest guide you'll ever come across, on how and why you should start investing as early as possible. In nine easy steps, I'll show you how to sidestep common beginner investment challenges and map the way forward as you work towards your financial success. You can think of this as your go-to do's and don'ts for first-time investors.

Get Started With a Brokerage Account

The first thing you need to start investing is a brokerage account. This will be your financial gateway to the world of investing. Note that brokerage accounts could attract fees that ultimately eat into your profits, so make sure you choose an account that's transparent on things like management fees and commissions to avoid nasty surprises later on.

Your brokerage account is your personal platform for buying and selling investments. This is where you execute all your investment transactions. Having a brokerage account gives you access to a wide range of investment options. You can choose from thousands of stocks, bonds, ETFs (exchange-traded funds), and other assets to build a diversified portfolio.

Your brokerage account also gives you access to valuable tools and resources to help you make smart investment decisions. These include research reports, market analysis, and educational materials to assist you in understanding different investment opportunities and strategies. With this information, you should be able to manage your investments efficiently. From your account, you can monitor your portfolio performance, track market trends, and make adjustments to your investments.

Lastly, a brokerage account also gives you access to liquidity. You can easily convert your investments into cash whenever you need it, enabling you to take advantage of opportunities in the market or get the cash you need to meet unexpected expenses.

Now that you understand the need for a brokerage account, here are some simple steps guiding on how to open one, and begin your journey to financial independence:

1. Research brokerage firms to understand the type of accounts they have, and their offerings, then choose one that best meets your needs.
2. Fill out the application form with your personal details, and decide on the type of account you want to open.
3. Submit ID documents to verify your identity.
4. Once the account is verified, decide which means you'll use to fund your account.
5. Carefully review and sign all necessary paperwork, then send your completed application and documents to the brokerage firm.
6. Wait for the firm to approve your application. Once approved, you'll get confirmation and your account details.

7. Log in, explore the investment options available, and start investing.

Remember to keep your account information secure and stay informed about the investment opportunities and risks associated with your chosen brokerage account. Happy investing!

The Easy 9-Step Guide to I.N.V.E.S.T.I.N.G.

Here's a simple 9-step guide to help you on your investment journey:

Step 1: I—Identify Goals

To clearly define your investment objectives, start by reaffirming the principles we outlined in Chapter 1—You're working towards being wealthy, not just being rich. This means prioritizing long-term financial stability and growth over short-term gains. Take some time to think about what you want to achieve financially. Consider both short-term and long-term goals. Ask yourself questions like:

- What do I want to accomplish with my investments?
- How much wealth do I want to accumulate?
- What time frame am I looking at for these goals?

Make sure the said goals are specific and measurable. Instead of vague aspirations like "I want to make money," specify targets such as:

- I want to achieve a certain level of passive income by the time I retire.
- I want to build a diversified investment portfolio worth $X by a particular date.
- I want to fund my children's education without relying on loans or scholarships.

As you draft these plans, think of how much risk you're comfortable with. Understand that higher potential returns typically come with higher risk. To this end, ask yourself the following questions:

- How would I react to market fluctuations?
- Can I afford to lose some or all of my investment in pursuit of higher returns?
- What is my investment horizon, and how does it affect my risk tolerance?

I'd also advise you to diversify your investments by spreading them across various asset classes to mitigate possible risks. This could include stocks, bonds, real estate, and alternative investments. Diversification helps protect your portfolio from the volatility of any single asset class. Remember that your personal values and any ethical or social considerations will come into play when choosing investments. You may prefer to invest in companies or funds that align with causes you believe in or avoid industries that conflict with your values.

Finally, remember that wealth is a long-term game, and that means being able to review and adjust your plans regularly. Your investment objectives may change over time due to changes in your financial situation, personal goals, or market conditions.

Step 2: N—Negotiate Finances

To assess your financial situation and determine how much you can invest without compromising daily needs and crucial savings, start by examining your monthly income and all your expenses. Make a list of all essential expenses, such as rent or mortgage, utilities, groceries, transportation, insurance, and debt repayments. On top of that, make sure you have a budget for discretionary spending on random things like dining out with the family, fun activities, entertainment, and shopping.

With this information, subtract your total monthly expenses from your monthly income to find out how much money you have left after covering your essentials. This is your disposable income—the amount you have available for saving and investing.

Before considering investments, it's always wise to set up and actively contribute to your savings and emergency fund. Try to set aside at least three to six months' worth of living expenses in an easily accessible savings account. This fund is your safety net in case of unexpected expenses or emergencies.

If you're new to investing or have limited funds available, don't feel pressured to invest a large sum right away. Start with a small amount that you're comfortable with, and gradually increase your investment contributions over time as your financial situation improves. To this end, I would advise you to set up a reasonable percentage of your disposable income that you're willing to allocate to investments each month. This could be anywhere from 5% to 20% or more, depending on your circumstances and goals. Make sure that this amount doesn't jeopardize your ability to meet your daily needs or contribute to essential savings.

Just like we mentioned in the previous section, this is a long-term plan, so you should create room in your plans to review and adjust your finances as your circumstances in life change over time.

Step 3: V—Verify Risk Tolerance

Understanding your risk tolerance is like knowing your own limits before embarking on a challenging journey. Just as a hiker assesses their endurance and ability before tackling a steep mountain trail, this is how you gauge how much volatility and uncertainty you can comfortably handle in your investment portfolio.

If you have a low-risk tolerance, you might prefer safer, more stable investments like bonds or blue-chip stocks. These investments may offer lower potential returns but come with less volatility and a reduced chance of losing your principal. On the other hand, if you have a higher risk tolerance, you might be willing to ride out market fluctuations in pursuit of potentially higher returns from riskier assets like growth stocks or emerging markets like cryptocurrency.

By understanding your risk tolerance, you can construct a well-balanced investment portfolio that reflects your financial goals. Knowing your limits will go a long way in helping you make smart investment decisions. It gives you the confidence to embrace your financial journey the right way. We will explore this concept in-depth in Chapter 4.

Step 4: E—Educate Yourself

Knowledge is power! This is particularly true in the investment business, because what you know goes a long way in helping you make smart and informed decisions about your financial future. Research allows you to identify opportunities that have the potential to generate higher returns. By diversifying your investment portfolio with a careful mix of assets, you can easily optimize your returns while managing risk.

This is also a good opportunity to learn about different investment options that align with your risk tolerance and financial goals. By understanding the characteristics and risks associated with each investment, you can mitigate the risk of potential losses and protect your capital. Risk management also means taking strategic measures to adapt your investment strategy to changing economic conditions. By monitoring market indicators, economic reports, and geopolitical events, you can anticipate market movements and adjust your portfolio accordingly to capitalize on emerging opportunities or mitigate potential risks.

The more you know about the market, the easier it is for you to approach investments confidently. When you have a solid understanding of the factors influencing the markets and the potential risks and rewards of different investments, you can invest with conviction, especially during periods of market volatility.

Step 5: S—Set a Budget

Establishing a realistic budget for your investments begins with a thorough assessment of your finances. This borrows a lot from the discussion we had earlier in the second point (Negotiate Finances). You need to know how much money you have coming in and how much is going out each month, setting the foundation for a budget that balances your investment goals with your day-to-day needs.

Once you have a clear understanding of your financial situation, it's essential to determine your investment goals and priorities to help you allocate your resources effectively, and create a plan that lays the groundwork for long-term financial success.

As you establish your investment budget, remember that life is dynamic, and your financial circumstances may change over time. A good budget should be flexible enough for you to make adjustments where necessary. That being said, you have to be careful not to be too flexible with your budget that it fails to serve your planning needs.

Step 6: T—Time Horizon for Entries and Exits

Consider how long you intend to invest when planning your investment strategy. Your time horizon—whether short-term or long-term—can significantly affect your approach and potential outcomes. Short-term investing typically means holding assets for a year or less, while long-term investing spans several years or decades.

Short-term investing offers the potential for quick gains, allowing you to capitalize on market fluctuations and take advantage of short-term opportunities. However, it also comes with higher volatility and increased risk. Market timing becomes crucial in short-term investing, as you must accurately predict market movements to achieve success. Pay close attention to market trends, economic indicators, and news events that may influence asset prices. Look for favorable entry points when prices are low or undervalued and consider setting clear exit points to lock in profits or limit losses.

On the other hand, long-term investing is ideal for steady growth and compounding returns over time. By taking a buy-and-hold approach, you can ride out market fluctuations and benefit from the power of compounding. Long-term investments tend to be less sensitive to short-term market volatility, allowing you to focus on the fundamental strength of your investments rather than short-term price movements. When investing for the long term, prioritize quality assets with strong fundamentals and a proven track record of growth. One of the most effective strategies, especially for beginner investors, is dollar-cost averaging. This allows you to smooth out market volatility and gradually build your positions over time.

Regardless of your time horizon, you must learn how to time your market entry and exit to maximize your investment returns. Conduct thorough research and analysis to identify great entry points for buying and exit points for selling different assets. Remember that every market has unique dynamics, so the factors that affect entry and exit points for stocks, for example, might not be the same for options trading.

Ideally, you should look for opportunities where asset prices are undervalued relative to their intrinsic value and future growth potential. Avoid emotional decision-making and stick to your investment plan, particularly when the market is highly volatile. We will explore more on this in Chapters 5-7.

Step 7: I—Invest Regularly

Regular and consistent contributions to your investment portfolio will go a long way in building long-term wealth and achieving your financial goals. By regularly investing a fixed amount of money over time, you can take advantage of dollar-cost averaging.

Consistent contributions help you smooth out market fluctuations and reduce the impact of timing the market. Instead of trying to predict the best time to invest, you spread your purchases over time, buying more shares when prices are low and fewer shares when prices are high. This disciplined approach helps mitigate the risk of investing a large sum of money all at once, which could leave you vulnerable to market volatility.

To take advantage of dollar-cost averaging, start by determining how much you can afford to invest regularly, whether it's monthly, quarterly, or annually. Set up automatic contributions from your bank account to your investment accounts to ensure consistency. By investing the same amount at regular intervals, you buy more shares when prices are low and fewer shares when prices are high, averaging out your cost per share over time.

For this approach to work, you must stick to your investment plan and avoid making emotional decisions, especially with respect to short-term market fluctuations. Bear in mind the fact that investing is a marathon rather than a sprint, so always plan with a long-term vision in mind. This calls for consistency and patience particularly in difficult market conditions, while focusing on your financial objectives.

Step 8: N—Never Put All Eggs in One Basket

Diversification is another important investment concept you should use to your advantage. The goal of a diversified portfolio is to spread risk and protect your financial assets. When you concentrate your investments on a single asset or sector, you expose yourself to higher levels of risk. If that particular asset or sector is struggling, your entire investment portfolio could suffer significant losses. Diversification is your best defense against this risk.

When you diversify your investments across various asset classes, industries, and geographic regions, you can easily protect your entire portfolio from the effect of a single investment struggling in the market. Diversification helps cushion your portfolio against market volatility and unexpected events, thereby increasing the likelihood of achieving consistent returns over time.

Resist the temptation to put all your eggs in one basket, no matter how promising a particular investment may seem. Instead, aim to build a well-diversified portfolio that includes a well-researched mix of assets. For example, you could spread your investments across various sectors like technology, healthcare, consumer goods, and finance.

Remember that diversification is not a guarantee that you will not make losses, but it does help manage risk and improve the stability of your investment portfolio. Diversification goes hand in hand with discipline, so you must still stay focused on your investment goals for the best chance of achieving financial security.

Step 9: G—Gauge Progress

The final step is to regularly monitor and evaluate your investments over time, a concept that we will discuss at length in Chapter 12. This evaluation is essential for maintaining a successful investment strategy. By staying vigilant and proactive, you can adapt to changing market conditions and ensure that your portfolio remains aligned with your financial goals throughout.

Gauging your progress over time helps you stay informed about market trends, economic indicators, and geopolitical events that may affect your portfolio. As you keep a close eye on your investments, you can identify potential opportunities and risks early on, making it easier to take appropriate action.

Evaluating your investments on a regular basis also helps you assess their performance relative to your financial goals and level of risk tolerance. As you analyze the returns, volatility, and overall health of your portfolio, you can easily determine whether adjustments are necessary to keep your investments on track.

If market conditions change or your financial goals evolve, don't hesitate to adjust your investment strategy accordingly. This might involve rebalancing your portfolio to maintain your desired asset allocation, reallocating investments to sectors or asset classes with better growth prospects, or even making strategic changes to your long-term investment plan. Whichever approach you choose, you should always remember that investing is a dynamic process, and flexibility is key to success.

As we wrap up this section, I'd wish to draw your attention to the discussion we had in the first chapter, on wealth vs. riches. The key to achieving wealth lies in setting clear, achievable objectives and sticking to a disciplined investment approach over time. These concepts are aptly captured in the steps we've outlined, and should help you stay focused on your long-term goals. Building on this, we now shift our attention to investment risks in the next chapter. We will discuss common risks that threaten the viability of your investments, and how to protect your investments against their inevitability.

CHAPTER 4:

The Risks in Investing, and How to Easily Conquer Them

When you make your first attempt into the financial markets, you're entering a world where uncertainty reigns supreme. Risk is a normal part of investment, and it is actually because of risk that some investments have the kind of amazing yields that many people boast of. The market can shift in an instant, leaving even the most seasoned investors scratching their heads in disbelief.

As you assess investment opportunities, remember that risks are always lurking around every corner. That seemingly foolproof stock? It could plummet in value overnight, leaving your portfolio in shambles. That promising new venture? It might encounter unforeseen obstacles that derail your plans.

The lesson here is that in the world of finance, there are no guarantees. No matter how meticulously you analyze the data or how confidently you make your decisions, the market can always throw you a curveball. It's a constant game of chance, where fortunes can be made or lost in an instant.

So, as you tread through the turbulence of financial markets, remember to proceed cautiously. Stay vigilant, diversify your investments, and always be prepared for the unexpected. Because in this unpredictable landscape, only the resilient and adaptable thrive.

There's Always a Risk

Risk represents the potential for loss, the uncertainty that keeps you on your toes in the financial markets. When you invest, you're essentially putting your money on the line with the hope of earning a return. But alongside that potential reward comes the looming possibility of risk. There's the chance that your investment might not pan out as expected and that external factors beyond your control could lead to losses.

Every investment decision you make involves a trade-off between risk and reward. Higher potential returns often come with higher levels of risk, while safer investments typically offer lower returns. It's a delicate balancing act, where you must weigh the potential gains against the possibility of loss.

Understanding risk is crucial for investors. It's not just about accepting it blindly, but rather about managing it effectively. Diversifying your portfolio, conducting thorough research, and staying informed about market trends are all strategies to help mitigate risk.

Ultimately, risk is an inherent part of investing. It's the factor that keeps the game interesting, the variable that adds excitement and challenge to the journey toward financial growth. Embrace it, but always approach it with caution and diligence, knowing that wise risk management is key to long-term success. While it's a fact that there's always a risk in investment, you can't just accept it and resign yourself to fate. The first, and most important step to conquering risk is usually to understand the kind of risks you are willing to take, and how much. Once you know those two, you are well on your way to making bold investment moves in the market.

What Risks Are You Willing to Take?

Your risk appetite is like a compass. It tells you a lot about your willingness to take calculated risks in the market with the hope of making some good returns. Risk appetite is influenced by different factors, including your financial goals, time horizon, and personal preferences. Are you willing to take bold risks in pursuit of high returns, or do you prefer to play it safe and opt for more conservative investments? Understanding your risk appetite is crucial because it helps you align your investment choices with your comfort level.

On the other hand, your risk tolerance is what protects you against the uncertainties of the market. It's your ability to withstand fluctuations in the value of your investments without losing sleep at night. Your risk tolerance is how you stay put when the market swings against you. You don't panic. Your risk tolerance is determined by factors like your financial situation, investment experience, and emotional resilience.

It's important to understand the fact that your risk appetite and risk tolerance may not always align perfectly. You might have a high-risk appetite but a low tolerance for volatility, or vice versa. The key is to strike a balance that allows you to pursue your financial goals.

Knowing your risk appetite and tolerance empowers you to make informed investment decisions that align with your personality and objectives. It's not about avoiding risk altogether but rather about recognizing and managing it intelligently to maximize your chances of success while minimizing potential stress and anxiety. So, take the time to assess your risk appetite and tolerance carefully—it could make all the difference in your investment journey.

Assessment 1

Use the assessment below to assess your level of risk tolerance.

Financial Goals

What are you working towards? (Clear goals usually indicate a higher risk tolerance).

Are your goals short-term, long-term, or a mix of both?

Investment Time Horizon

What is your investment time horizon? (Longer horizons generally align with higher risk tolerance)

Are you investing for retirement, a major purchase, or other specific goals?

Market Knowledge

How well do you understand different investment options? (A good understanding may suggest a higher level of risk tolerance)

Are you willing to learn more about investment strategies and markets?

Income Stability

How stable is your current source of income? (Stable income generally allows for a higher risk tolerance)

Do you have an emergency fund to cover unexpected expenses?

Emotional Resilience

How do you typically react to market fluctuations? (Calm and patient reactions may indicate a higher risk tolerance)

Can you withstand short-term losses without feeling significant stress?

Risk Capacity

What is your overall financial situation? (A stronger financial position may suggest a higher risk capacity)

Do you have debts or outstanding financial obligations?

Diversification

Are you comfortable diversifying your investments across different asset classes? (Diversification can impact risk tolerance)

How much concentration do you prefer in your investment portfolio?

Risk Preference

Do you prefer stability and capital preservation over potential higher returns?

Are you willing to accept higher volatility for the possibility of greater returns?

Life Stage

What life stage are you in? (Younger individuals often have a higher risk tolerance)

Have you considered how life events (e.g., marriage, children) might affect your risk tolerance? Elaborate further, especially on your fears or concerns around the said life events.

Risk Assessment Tools

Have you used any risk assessment tools provided by financial institutions or professionals?

Do the results of such tools align with your own perception of risk tolerance?

After considering these questions, you should have a better understanding of your risk appetite and level of risk tolerance. Keep in mind that your risk tolerance may evolve over time, so you'll need to periodically take this test as things change in your life, your financial situation, and your life goals.

Assessment 2

The exercise below will help you assess your financial situation and determine how much you can invest with the least risks involved, that is, without compromising your daily needs and crucial savings.

Step 1: Budget Analysis—Income and Expense Assessment

Make a detailed list of all your sources of income, including your salary, bonuses, freelance work, etc.

List your fixed monthly expenses such as rent/mortgage, utilities, insurance, loan payments, and groceries.

Identify variable expenses like dining out, entertainment, and shopping.

Confirm the balance in your emergency fund. This fund should cover 3–6 months of living expenses.

List your outstanding debts, including credit cards, loans, etc.

Step 2: Assessing Surplus Income

Subtract your total monthly expenses from your income to determine your surplus.

From your surplus, identify discretionary income (money available for non-essential spending).

Step 3: Establish Investment Budget

Clearly define your investment goals, whether it's for retirement, a home purchase, or other objectives.

Review your emergency fund to ensure it is sufficient. If not, prioritize topping it up before considering investments.

Allocate a portion of your surplus to accelerate debt repayment. This frees up your money for future investments.

Decide what percentage of your discretionary income you're comfortable investing. Start with a conservative figure, considering the risk tolerance assessment we did earlier.

Step 4: Risk Tolerance Check

Revisit the risk tolerance self-assessment to ensure your investment choices align with your comfort level.

Step 5: Monitor and Adjust

Periodically review your budget and investment strategy. Adjust as needed based on changes in income, expenses, or financial goals.

Ensure your emergency fund remains adequate, especially if there are significant life changes. How do you need to adjust accordingly?

As your financial situation improves, consider gradually increasing your investment percentage. For example, let's say you are working with a monthly surplus of $500 and decide to allocate 20% to investments, that's $100 per month. Make sure this adjustment does not jeopardize your essential needs or emergency fund requirements.

Even as you work through this plan, remember that it's a long-term process, so you will have to start small, stay within your comfort zone, and gradually increase your investment as your financial situation changes. Where necessary, engage a financial advisor for personalized advice as your circumstances change in life.

Types of Investment Risks

Building on the explanation above, here are some of the major investment risks that you could encounter in your investment life cycle:

Market Risk

Market risk, also known as systematic risk, refers to the risk of losses due to factors affecting the overall performance of the financial markets. These factors include economic conditions, geopolitical events, interest rate changes, and market sentiment.

You can manage market risk by diversifying your investments and spreading risk across different sectors. By spreading your investments across different asset classes, industries, and geographic regions, you can effectively reduce the impact of adverse market movements on your portfolio. You could also invest in assets with low correlation to each other to mitigate market risk.

Credit Risk

Credit risk arises from the possibility that the issuer of a bond or debt instrument may default on interest or principal payments. It's particularly relevant when you're investing in corporate bonds, municipal bonds, or other fixed-income securities.

To manage credit risk, diversify your fixed-income holdings across issuers with different credit ratings. Investing in government bonds or high-quality corporate bonds can also reduce your exposure to credit risk. Additionally, it's always advisable to stay informed about the financial health and creditworthiness of issuers through credit ratings and financial analysis. This gives you useful information to make bold moves, especially when it comes to balancing your investment portfolio.

Liquidity Risk

Liquidity risk refers to the risk of not being able to buy or sell an investment quickly and at a fair price. It typically arises in less liquid markets or with assets that have low trading volumes. For example, you might struggle to sell a house faster compared to selling stocks.

Diversification is one way to indirectly mitigate liquidity risk by ensuring that your portfolio includes liquid assets that can be easily bought or sold. Avoid investments with limited trading volumes. Another solution for this risk is to invest in exchange-traded funds (ETFs) and mutual funds, which usually provide liquidity through secondary markets.

Inflation Risk

Inflation risk, also known as purchasing power risk, is the risk that the real value of your investments will decline over time due to rising inflation eroding the purchasing power of your money. Inflation risk is a common problem, not just in the investment space, but also in savings and other aspects of your finances. For example, if you open a savings account, there's always a risk that the amount of interest you earn from the savings account might be lower than the rate of inflation. In that case, you're effectively losing money by saving it in that account.

To hedge against inflation risk, consider investing in assets that have historically provided returns that outpace inflation. These include investments in equities, real estate, and inflation-protected securities like Treasury Inflation-Protected Securities (TIPS). I would also advise you to regularly review and adjust your investment strategy to account for changes in inflation. It's all about managing your expectations.

Currency Risk

Currency risk is also known as exchange rate risk. This risk comes from fluctuations in exchange rates between different currencies. It's particularly relevant if you hold assets denominated in different foreign currencies.

Since there are multiple currencies involved, there's so much at play that you might not be able to control. This is why diversification is always a smart move to hedge against currency risk. Consider investing in assets denominated in different currencies or using currency hedging techniques. Good examples include forward contracts or currency options, which reduce exposure to adverse currency movements.

As long as you're holding investments in different currencies, you'll need to learn about the macroeconomic factors and geopolitical events that influence exchange rates in the relevant countries. This goes a long way in helping you manage currency risk effectively.

Looking at the potential risks above, it's clear that diversification remains an important strategy for protecting your investments. By spreading your investments across a range of assets with different risk profiles, you can reduce the impact of individual risks on your overall portfolio. Note, however, that diversification is not a guarantee that you will eliminate risk entirely. Instead, it can help you mitigate the impact of specific risk factors, giving you a more stable foundation for long-term investment success.

A Budget for Your Investments

Creating a budget for your investments is one of the most important steps in achieving your financial goals. We talk about budgets all the time, but not so much about how to go about building them in the first place. Here are some simple steps to help you get started:

1. Start by evaluating your current financial status. Consider your income, including wages, bonuses, and any other sources of revenue. Then, deduct your monthly expenses, such as rent or mortgage, utilities, groceries, transportation, and debt payments. This will give you a clear picture of how much disposable income you have available for investment.
2. Once you know your financial position, work on your goals. What are you working towards? Figure out what you want to achieve with your investments, and set specific, measurable, achievable, relevant, and time-bound (SMART) goals to help you stay focused and motivated. Your goals will then inform your investment budget.
3. Decide how much of your income you're willing to allocate towards investments every month. This amount should be based on your financial goals, risk tolerance, and current and future financial obligations. Try to strike a balance between investing just enough to make meaningful progress toward your goals and maintaining a comfortable standard of living. You don't want to end up sacrificing so much of your money that you live an unnecessarily miserable life.
4. In case you have high-interest debt, consider prioritizing debt repayment before allocating a significant portion of your budget to investments. High-interest debt includes payments like credit card balances or personal loans. Paying off such debt can provide a guaranteed return on your money by reducing interest expenses and improving your financial health.
5. As you work on this plan, remember to set up an emergency fund to protect yourself against selling your investments at a loss to raise some quick funds for an emergency. Your emergency fund covers unexpected expenses or financial setbacks, and should ideally be worth three to six months' worth of living expenses in a liquid, easily accessible account, such as a high-yield savings account or a money market fund.

You're almost set, so figure out the ideal investment opportunities that align with your financial goals and level of risk tolerance. Most people start with investments like stocks, bonds, mutual funds, exchange-traded funds, real estate, and retirement accounts like 401(k)s or IRAs. However, you don't necessarily have to limit yourself to such. You could also explore riskier options like cryptocurrency, but only if you are certain you can handle the pressure that comes with it.

Once your budget is set, spare time to regularly review it, and make adjustments according to your portfolio performance. The goal here is to make sure that your investments are always aligned with your financial goals and risk tolerance. Your budget should act as a guide, one that helps you make adjustments with respect to changes in your immediate circumstances.

Ultimately, creating an investment budget is just the first step. A lot of factors come into play, which will determine whether your investment approach becomes a success or not. These include consistency, discipline, and patience. More importantly, you must learn to manage your expectations, and avoid becoming emotionally invested in your approach.

Assessment 3

Here's a simple worksheet that you can use as a guide to create your investment budget plan. This worksheet aligns with the principles discussed earlier in the self-assessment exercise. Remember to customize the values based on your own financial situation and goals.

Step 1: Budget Analysis

Income Assessment

Salary:

$

Bonuses/Additional income:

$

Total income = Salary + bonuses and additional income

$

Expense Assessment: Fixed Expenses

Rent/Mortgage:

$

Utilities:

$

Insurance:

$

Loan payments:

$

Groceries:

$

Other fixed expenses:

$

Total fixed expenses = Sum of all the fixed expenses listed above

$

Expense Assessment: Variable Expenses

Dining out:

$

Entertainment:

$

Shopping:

$

Any other variable expenses:

$

Total variable expenses = Sum of all the variable expenses listed above

$

Emergency fund balance

$

Debt Assessment

Credit card payments:

$

Loan payments:

$

Other debts:

$

Total debts = Sum of all the debts listed above

$

Step 2: Assessing Surplus Income

Monthly surplus = Total income − (Total fixed expenses + Total variable expenses + Total debts)

$

Identify Discretionary Income (Income used for non-essential expenditure)

$

Step 3: Establish Investment Budget

Define and list your investment goals, and the amounts you need for them, as shown. This could be anything from retirement, buying a home, tuition, etc.

Home purchase - $500,000

School - $200,000

Is the Emergency Fund sufficient? If not, how much funds do you need to top it up?

$

Debt Repayment

How much of your surplus income can you allocate to speed up your debt repayment?

$

Monthly Investment Budget

Decide the percentage of discretionary income for investments (e.g., 20%).

Monthly investment budget = Discretionary Income x Investment Percentage

$

Step 4: Risk Tolerance Check

Ensure your investment plan aligns with your risk tolerance as assessed earlier. What aspects of your investment plan are a perfect fit for your level of risk tolerance?

What aspects of your investment plan need adjustment to fit your level of risk tolerance?

Step 5: Monitor and Adjust

- Periodically review your budget and adjust as needed.
- Ensure the Emergency Fund remains adequate.
- As your financial situation improves, consider increasing the investment percentage.

Remember that this assessment is not definite, but should only act as a guide to help you customize your plans according to your financial situation. Feel free to tweak it to suit your lifestyle, and where possible, engage a financial advisor to help you tailor your plan according to your circumstances. Ambition is good, but the last thing you want is a plan that's too ambitious that it defeats its core purpose.

PART II:

The Three Giants of Investments

CHAPTER 5:

Stocks: Demystifying the Art of Equity Investment

Stock market investments come up in conversations from time to time. You've probably engaged in some of these conversations at some point in your life—perhaps in casual conversations when you're watching the financial news, or even from that friend who can never shut up about their exploits in the market. To be fair, the stock market is a topic that's omnipresent today, and you might have even entertained the idea of diving into it yourself. However, have you truly considered what it means to be an investor, and have you pondered how these markets can shape your financial future? That's what this chapter is about, transforming your passive curiosity into active engagement, your fleeting interest into a solid foundation for financial success.

Whether you're looking to build wealth for the long term, save for a specific goal, or simply make your money work harder for you, this chapter is your compass in navigating the stock market, with fundamental knowledge, strategic insights, and practical tips to kickstart your investment journey and empower you to make smart investment decisions.

My goal is that by the end of this chapter, you won't just be a spectator in the world of finance; you'll be an active participant, steering your financial destiny with confidence, from investing in your first stocks to achieving your ultimate financial goals.

Investing in the Stock Market

Before we talk about how to invest in the stock market, let's explore the fundamentals—what is this market all about? More importantly, what is a stock?

A stock represents your share of ownership in a company. When you own a share of stock, you own a piece of that company. This means that if you buy stocks in Apple, NVIDIA, or any other company listed on the stock exchange, you own a fraction of that company proportionate to the amount of stocks you own. Companies issue stocks to raise capital for different reasons, for example, to fund expansion, research, or debt repayment. In return, you, the investor, become a shareholder and may receive a portion of the company's profits in the form of dividends.

The stock market is a platform where buyers and sellers come together to trade ownership shares in publicly traded companies. It acts as a marketplace for investors to buy and sell stocks. Through the stock market, companies can raise capital by issuing stocks for sale, which offers investors the opportunity to potentially profit from the growth of those companies. Prices of stocks are determined by supply and demand dynamics, as well as various factors such as company performance, economic conditions, and investor sentiment. Some famous stock markets include the New York Stock Exchange (NYSE), the Nasdaq in the United States, the London Stock Exchange (LSE), and the Tokyo Stock Exchange (TSE).

Building on the basics above, let's dive deeper and explore how stocks work.

First, you'll need to open a brokerage account to buy stocks. Stocks are bought and sold based on supply and demand. If more people want to buy a stock (demand), its price tends to rise. On the other hand, if more people want to sell (supply), the price may fall. Changes in stock prices are influenced by different factors, including company performance, economic conditions, industry trends, and global events.

Some companies pay dividends after a period of strong financial performance. Dividends are payments made by a company to its shareholders out of its earnings or profits at the end of a trading period. These payments are typically distributed periodically, often quarterly, although some companies may pay dividends annually or semi-annually. Dividends are one way for companies to share their financial success with shareholders. It's good to point out that not all stocks pay dividends. In some cases, you might choose to focus on growth stocks that reinvest profits into the company instead of issuing dividends.

So, given what we know so far, you're probably wondering how you eventually make money from owning stocks. Apart from dividends that we mentioned earlier, you can make money through capital gains. This is where you make money by selling the stocks at a higher price than you bought them. Note that if you earn such a profit, you'll have to pay capital gains taxes.

Success in the stock market requires research and staying informed about the market and specific companies. You must also learn how to interpret financial reports, economic indicators, and industry trends to help you make informed investment decisions.

Why Invest in the Stock Market?

It's clear from our discussion above that the stock market can be an amazing investment opportunity. The prospect of dividends and capital gains gives you something to be excited about. However, there's more to the stock market than that. Here are some reasons why investors, both individuals and companies, like to put their money in the stock market.

- **Capital Formation:** The stock market is a good place for companies to raise capital. When a company goes public by issuing stocks through an initial public offering (IPO), it allows investors to buy shares and become partial owners. The money raised from selling these shares gives the company additional capital that's more affordable than if they had to go to a bank for a loan.

- **Liquidity**: The ease with which you can buy or sell shares on the stock exchange means your investments are relatively liquid, compared to investing in something like real estate that cannot be easily offloaded.
- **Employee Incentives**: Some companies use stocks as incentives for employees. Offering employees the opportunity to own a stake in the company aligns their interests with the company's success. This way, employees contribute to the company's growth and success, fostering a sense of ownership and motivation to contribute to the company's long-term success.
- **Wealth Accumulation**: The stock market is a means of accumulating wealth over time. Historically, the stock market has provided attractive returns, outpacing inflation and other investment options. As an investor seeking capital appreciation through stock price appreciation and dividends allows you to grow your wealth and achieve financial goals such as, early retirement, tuition, or any other long-term objectives.

The Pros and Cons of Stocks

Here are some benefits you could enjoy by investing in stocks:

- Stocks generally have high returns if you invest over the long term. Investing in well-performing stocks can outpace other forms of investment, such as bonds or your savings account.
- You become a part owner of the companies you invest in. As a shareholder, you may have voting rights on certain company decisions.

- Stocks are generally liquid assets, making it easier for you to react quickly to market conditions or changes in your financial circumstances.
- Investing in a variety of stocks across different sectors and industries allows for portfolio diversification. This strategy helps you spread risk, as poor performance in one sector may be offset by gains in another.
- Stocks have the potential for long-term growth, especially when you invest in fundamentally strong companies. If you are patient and hold onto your investments through market fluctuations, you might benefit from overall market growth in the long run.

The points above present the stock market as an exciting investment opportunity. However, you must also be aware of the possible risks of investing in this market. Note that in the business world, there's always a risk in every investment. Here are some risks you should be aware of:

- Stocks are subject to market volatility, and their prices can fluctuate significantly. This volatility introduces risk, so there is a possibility of losing a portion or all of your invested capital.
- Unlike fixed-income investments like bonds, stocks do not always guarantee returns. Stock prices depend on various factors, and for that reason, there's no certainty that you will profit from your investment.
- Economic and geopolitical events can affect stock prices, creating uncertainty in the market. Factors such as economic recession, political instability, or global crises like the COVID-19 pandemic can adversely affect stock values.
- Successful investments require lots of time and research. Apart from that, you must constantly monitor market conditions. This can be time-consuming, not to mention the fact that you

must also learn about the companies you wish to invest in, industry trends, and economic indicators.

- Market fluctuations and downturns can evoke emotional responses, leading to impulsive decision-making. Emotional reactions, for example, panic selling during market downturns, may drive you to make losses.

Ultimately, even though the relevant authorities in the stock market try to keep things running above board, the stock market is not immune to manipulation and fraudulent activities. From insider trading and pump-and-dump schemes to misinformation, you might fall victim to some of these activities that affect stock prices, and make an unnecessary move in the market that costs you dearly.

Stock Market Trends

Long-term trends in the stock market are the sustained directional movements of stock prices over an extended period of time. By long-term, we're talking about trends spanning years or decades. These trends are characterized by the general trajectory of the market, reflecting the overall performance and growth of the stock market over time. Long-term trends are generally influenced by a number of factors, including economic conditions, technological advancements, demographic shifts, and geopolitical events.

Long-term trends often show an overall upward trajectory, indicating the general growth and expansion of the stock market. Despite short-term fluctuations and occasional downturns, the market tends to exhibit positive momentum over extended periods. They could also be influenced by economic cycles such as long periods of expansion and contraction in the economy. Bull markets, characterized by rising stock prices, are often associated with economic expansion, while bear markets, marked by declining prices, may coincide with economic downturns.

To make smart moves around market trends, you must consider factors such as historical performance, economic outlook, and fundamental indicators. Long-term trend analysis can help you investors devise a broader perspective on the market and adjust your investment strategies to align with anticipated future developments in the stock market.

Let's look at some common economic signs that the market might be riding the wave of a long-term trend:

Period of Sustained Growth

One of the prominent long-term trends in the stock market is its overall growth. Despite short-term fluctuations, the stock market has displayed a general upward trajectory over extended periods. This growth is often driven by economic expansion, technological advancements, and increased productivity across various industries. A good example of this is the COVID-19 pandemic, when stock markets were depressed all over the world, but soon bounced back. Soon after that, the market struggled amid the recession, the effect of the Russia-Ukraine war, the ongoing conversation about de-dollarizing the global economy, and fluctuating oil prices, but despite the upheavals, the stock market still found its balance.

Try to learn as much as possible about key economic indicators like GDP growth, employment rates, and inflation. Positive economic trends are usually a sign of a favorable environment for stock investments. You should also keep a close eye on companies' financial health and earnings reports. Strong earnings growth is often a positive sign for stock prices. Look for companies that have consistently turned profits over the years.

Technological Innovation

Technological innovation has been a consistent driver of long-term stock market trends. Historical examples include the impact of the internet in the 1990s and the rise of technology giants like Google, Meta Platforms (formerly Facebook), NVIDIA, and Apple in recent decades. When companies at the forefront of technological advancements experience significant growth, the stock market in general usually enjoys the spillover effect, resulting in overall market growth.

Your best move is to identify companies at the forefront of technological innovation. You'll realize that there are lots of growth opportunities in industries that are embracing technological advancements, for example, artificial intelligence, renewable energy, and biotechnology.

Significant Demographic Shifts

Changes in the demographic makeup can trigger long-term shifts in the market. For example, adverse changes in population growth, aging populations, and shifts in consumer behavior play a role in shaping long-term stock market trends. Take the example of industries related to healthcare, senior services, and technology catering to changing consumer preferences. Growth in these sectors is often in response to demographic changes.

Environmental, Social, and Governance (ESG) Trends

There has been a growing emphasis on ESG factors in the stock market. Investors increasingly consider a company's environmental impact, social responsibility, and governance policies when conducting due diligence prior to their investment. Companies that follow sustainable and ethical practices attract investors seeking both financial returns and positive contributions to society.

In your market research, prioritize companies with strong ESG practices, particularly on sustainability and ethical considerations. Besides, investing in companies that are committed to ESG principles may align with broader market trends.

Knowledge of these long-term trends will go a long way in helping you make informed decisions and successfully navigate the complexities of the stock market.

The trends we've discussed won't always apply throughout the stock market. In some cases, you'll notice that some industries stay strong while others struggle. For that reason, you need to be smart in the kind of strategies you implement to leverage the factors that influence shifts in market trends.

Your knowledge of market trends notwithstanding, one of the most important skills that will drive your success in the stock market is to conquer your emotions. The market is dynamic, so you must try and avoid emotional decision-making, especially when the fluctuations go against your expectations. Stick to your investment strategy and resist the urge to make impulsive moves during times of market volatility.

The Major Market Indices

Market indices, often referred to simply as indices, are statistical measures that represent the performance of a specific segment of the financial market. They serve as benchmarks or indicators that investors use to assess the overall direction and health of the market, industry, or the economy in general. Given their range, you can also use indicators as a reference point for evaluating the performance of individual investments or your portfolio in general.

Let's briefly explore the S&P 500, Nasdaq Composite, and Dow Jones Industrial Average (DJIA), the three major stock market indices in the United States that you should know about. Each of these indices provides a snapshot of the overall performance of different segments of the market.

S&P 500

The Standard & Poor's 500 (S&P 500), is a market-capitalization-weighted index that represents the performance of 500 of the largest publicly traded companies in the US. There are companies in various sectors and industries, making the S&P 500 a broad and diverse measure of the U.S. stock market. Due to its broad composition, it provides a more comprehensive view of market trends compared to narrower indices. You can use the S&P 500 index funds or exchange-traded funds (ETFs) to gain exposure to a diversified portfolio of large-cap stocks.

Nasdaq Composite

The Nasdaq Composite includes more than 3,000 companies listed on the Nasdaq stock exchange. It heavily represents technology and internet-related companies, including giants like Apple, Amazon, Microsoft, and Google's parent company, Alphabet. Given its make-up, it's mostly a growth-oriented index, a barometer for the performance of technology and innovation stocks.

Dow Jones Industrial Average (DJIA)

The Dow Jones Industrial Average is a price-weighted index that includes 30 large, blue-chip U.S. companies. It represents a diverse range of industries, including technology, healthcare, finance, and manufacturing. However, it is a smaller and more selective index compared to the S&P 500. Being a price-weighted index, it gives higher-priced stocks more influence, regardless of their market capitalization. The DJIA is considered by some as a measure of the "old economy," with a focus on established and well-known companies.

Which Is the Best Investment?

Determining which index is the best investment of these indices depends on your financial goals, risk tolerance, and investment strategy because each index has some unique strengths and weaknesses. Generally, you can think of the indices in the following manner:

- S&P 500 offers broad market exposure and is suitable for diversified, long-term investments.
- Nasdaq Composite appeals to investors seeking exposure to technology and growth stocks, with potential for higher

volatility, which makes it ideal if you have a high appetite for risk.

- The Dow Jones Industrial Average represents a more selective group of large, established companies, but may not provide as diverse a portfolio as the S&P 500.

The fact is that there is no one-size-fits-all choice of the three. If anything, many investors choose to diversify by investing in a combination of these indices or other asset classes. Index funds or ETFs tracking these three indices are popular choices in case you are looking for passive, broad market exposure. That being said, you should always align your investment choices with your financial goals, risk tolerance, and investment time horizon.

Step-by-Step Guide to Investing in Stocks

Congratulations on taking a bold first step towards building your wealth through investing in stocks. Before we proceed, there are two important things I'd love to highlight, the time horizon and the role of regular contributions.

Consider your time horizon when investing in stocks. If you have a long time horizon, you can afford to take on more risk and invest in higher-growth stocks. For shorter time horizons, focus on more stable, dividend-paying stocks.

To ease the investment journey, try and make regular contributions to your portfolio. A common method for this is known as dollar-cost averaging. By investing a fixed amount regularly, you can take advantage of market fluctuations and potentially lower your average cost per share over time.

The steps below will guide you through the process of investing in stocks, including associated costs, risks, and strategies to mitigate them.

- **Step 1—Learning**: Before diving into the world of stocks, it's essential to educate yourself. Understand the basics of how the stock market works, different investment strategies, and how to analyze stocks.

- **Step 2—Your investment vision**: Define your investment goals. Are you investing for retirement, to buy a house or for other financial goals? Understanding your objectives will help shape your investment strategy.
- **Step 3—Risk assessment**: Consider your risk tolerance. How much volatility can you handle in your investment portfolio? Understanding your risk tolerance will guide you in selecting appropriate stocks that match your risk preference.
- **Step 4—Open a brokerage account**: You'll need to open a brokerage account. Choose a reputable brokerage platform that suits your needs and offers reasonable fees and commissions.
- **Step 5—Research and select stocks**: Do thorough research on the stocks you're interested in. Look into the company's financial health, management team, industry trends, and growth prospects.
- **Step 6—Place your orders**: Once you've selected the stocks you want to invest in, place your buy orders through your brokerage account. You can buy stocks at the current market price or set limit orders to buy at a specific price.

When investing in stocks, be aware of the associated costs, including brokerage commissions, taxes on capital gains, and any management fees if you're investing through mutual funds or ETFs. Since these usually eat into your profits, it’s wise to select brokerage accounts that are transparent with you in terms of the costs they charge your account, and the transactions.

Stock market investing comes with inherent risks. To mitigate these risks, diversify your portfolio across different stocks and industries, invest for the long term, and try to stay informed about market trends and economic developments. You should particularly be on the lookout for stock splits, a situation where a company divides its existing shares into multiple shares. For example, in a 2-for-1 stock split, each existing share becomes two shares. Stock splits don't change the overall value of your investment but can affect liquidity and trading volume.

Throughout this chapter, we emphasized the need and importance of goal-setting and risk management in your approach to investment. These concepts are fundamental to successful investing and apply not only to stock market investing but also to other types of investments. In the next chapter, we'll delve into the world of bonds, which are debt securities issued by governments, municipalities, or corporations. Understanding bonds will provide you with a well-rounded knowledge of investment options and help you diversify your portfolio effectively.

CHAPTER 6:

Bonds:
Decoding the World of Debt Securities

—♦—

For most people who are just getting started with investments, investing in bonds always seems like something reserved for adults or seasoned professionals. However, that's far from the truth. Bonds can be a valuable asset for anyone looking to grow their wealth and secure their financial future, regardless of age or experience. In this chapter, we'll break down complex financial concepts around bond investments into clear, manageable steps, ensuring that you not only understand how bonds work but also feel confident in incorporating them into your investment strategy.

As you read this chapter, I once again implore you to start as early as possible, start where you are. Bonds are some of the safest investment instruments in the financial sector, so don't wait until you save up a lot of money. By the end of this chapter, I hope that you will not only have a solid understanding of bond investments but also feel empowered to seek out bond investments that suit your portfolio allocation.

Investing in Bonds

Bonds are essentially loans that investors issue to governments, municipalities, corporations, or whichever other entity that offers the bond. When you invest in a bond, you are lending money to the issuer for a predetermined period of time, during which the issuer pays you periodic interest payments, typically semiannually or annually, known as coupon payments. At the end of the bond's term, known as the maturity date, the issuer repays the initial amount borrowed, known as the principal or face value. You can make money from bond investments in the following ways:

- **Interest Income (Coupon Payments)**: The primary way investors make money from bonds is through the interest payments, or coupon payments, that the issuer makes to bondholders. These payments are typically fixed and determined at the time of issuance based on the bond's coupon rate and face value. For example, if you invest $1,000 in a bond with a 5% coupon rate, you'll receive $50 in interest payments annually ($1,000 * 0.05).
- **Capital Appreciation**: Bond prices fluctuate in response to changes in interest rates, market conditions, and the issuer's creditworthiness. If interest rates fall after you've purchased a bond, the bond's market value will likely increase because its fixed interest payments become more attractive relative to newly issued bonds with lower coupon rates. You can then sell the bond at a higher price than you paid, realizing a capital gain. On the other hand, if interest rates rise, bond prices may fall, resulting in a capital loss if you sell the bond before maturity.
- **Discount or Premium Bonds**: When you buy a bond below its face value, it's called a discount bond. For instance, if you buy a $1,000 bond for $900, you're getting it at a discount. When the bond matures, you receive the full face value of $1,000, resulting in a capital gain. If you buy a bond above its face value, it's called a premium bond. In this case, you pay more than the face value upfront, but you'll still receive the face value at maturity. The difference between the purchase price and the face value represents your capital loss.

- **Yield to Maturity (YTM)**: YTM is the total return you can expect to receive if you hold the bond until it matures, factoring in both the interest payments and any capital gains or losses. YTM takes into account the bond's current market price, coupon rate, and time to maturity. YTM provides a standardized measure for comparing the potential returns of different bonds.

As you can see, there are different ways for you to make money by investing in bonds. You must, however, pay attention to factors like interest rate risk, credit risk, and inflation risk when selecting bonds, because these determine the profitability of the investment, and more importantly, this could also have an impact on your investment goals. Here are the major bond types you should be aware of:

- **Government Bonds**: Government bonds are issued by national governments to finance their operations or projects, and include Treasury bonds (issued by the U.S. government), as well as bonds issued by other governments worldwide. They are typically considered low-risk investments due to the backing of the government's taxing power, making them popular among conservative investors.

- **Municipal Bonds**: Municipal bonds are issued by state and local governments or their agencies to fund public projects such as schools, roads, and infrastructure. Interest income from municipal bonds is often exempt from federal income taxes and may also be exempt from state and local taxes if you reside in the issuing municipality.

- **Corporate Bonds**: Corporate bonds are issued by companies to raise capital for various purposes, for example, expansion, acquisitions, or refinancing existing debt. Their yields are usually higher than government bonds to compensate investors for the added risk associated with corporate creditworthiness.

- **High-Yield Bonds (Junk Bonds)**: High-yield bonds are issued by companies with lower credit ratings or higher risk of default. Their yields are higher because of the increased credit risk, making them attractive if you are looking for higher income potential.
- **Convertible Bonds**: Convertible bonds are an opportunity to convert your bond holdings into a predetermined number of the issuer's common stock shares. The potential upside of these bonds is participation in the issuer's equity appreciation while providing downside protection through their fixed-income characteristics.
- **International Bonds**: International bonds are issued by foreign governments or corporations and are denominated in currencies other than the investor's domestic currency. They provide diversification benefits and exposure to global markets but also come with a number of currency risks and the possibility of geopolitical interruptions.

Building on this, let's discuss the difference between individual bonds and bond funds:

Individual Bonds and Bond Funds

Individual bonds are securities issued by a single issuer with a fixed maturity date, coupon rate, and face value. You buy individual bonds directly from the issuer or on the secondary market through brokerage firms. Such bonds offer predictable cash flows, known maturity dates, and the potential for capital appreciation if you hold them to maturity. When you buy these bonds, you assume full control over the selection, purchase, and management, so you can practically adjust your portfolio to specific investment objectives and risk preferences.

Bond funds, on the other hand, operate like investment funds. They pool investors' money to invest in a diversified portfolio of bonds managed by professional portfolio managers. If you invest in these, you get instant diversification across various bond types, issuers, and maturities, reducing individual credit and interest rate risk. Bond funds may be actively managed, with portfolio managers actively selecting and trading bonds to achieve optimal returns, or passively managed, tracking a specific bond index. One of the main benefits of investing in bond funds is access to professional management, liquidity, and convenience. Note, however, that you may also incur management fees and expenses associated with fund ownership.

Factors that Influence Bond Prices

Even though bond prices are predetermined at the point of purchase, there are several factors you should be aware of, which usually determine the prices. These factors cut across both the primary market (at the point of issuance) and the secondary market (purchased after the bond has been issued). Knowledge of these factors goes a long way in shaping your investment agenda. Here are some of the major factors that determine bond prices:

- **Interest Rates**: Changes in prevailing interest rates have a significant impact on bond prices. When interest rates rise, newly issued bonds offer higher yields, making existing bonds with lower coupon rates less attractive. As a result, the prices of existing bonds fall to match the higher yields available in the market. On the flip side, when interest rates fall, existing bonds with higher coupon rates become more valuable, leading to an increase in bond prices.
- **Credit Quality**: The creditworthiness of the bond issuer usually affects bond prices. Bonds issued by entities with higher credit ratings, for example, government bonds or highly rated corporate bonds, are perceived as less risky and typically trade at higher prices than bonds with lower credit ratings like high-yield or junk bonds. Note that any changes to the issuer's credit rating or perceived credit risk could affect bond prices.

- **Economic Indicators**: Economic indicators such as inflation rates, GDP growth, unemployment rates, and consumer sentiment can also influence bond prices. For example, the expectation of higher inflation may lead to an increase in bond yields, causing bond prices to decline. On the other hand, signs of economic weakness or deflationary pressures may result in lower bond yields and higher bond prices as investors seek the safety of fixed-income assets.

- **Supply and Demand Economics**: Bond prices are also influenced by the dynamics of supply and demand in the market. Increased demand for bonds, either due to risk aversion or regulatory requirements, can drive up bond prices. Meanwhile, excess supply of bonds, for example in periods of heavy issuance or selling pressure, can depress bond prices.

- **Market Sentiment**: Investor sentiment and market psychology play an important role when determining bond prices. Positive market sentiment could lead investors to pursue riskier assets, causing bond prices to fall. Negative sentiment or uncertainty, on the other hand, may drive investors to seek safer assets like bonds, pushing prices higher.

- **Yield Curve**: The shape of the yield curve, which represents the relationship between bond yields and maturities, can influence bond prices. Changes in the yield curve, for example, steepening or flattening, reflect a shift in market expectations on future interest rates and economic conditions. These ultimately affect bond prices.

- **Currency Exchange Rates**: This applies to international bonds, especially those that are denominated in foreign currencies. Forex fluctuations will affect the prices of such bonds especially if you are holding them in your domestic currency. Changes in exchange rates relative to your base currency can impact the effective returns and attractiveness of international bonds.

The Highs and Lows of Bond Investments

Like every other investment market, the bond market has its ups and downs. Knowledge of this can help you capitalize on the benefits, while taking precautions not to be grossly disadvantaged by lows. This is why some people consider knowledge of the market to be a risk mitigation approach. Here are some of the benefits of investing in the bond market:

- Bonds offer a stable source of income through regular interest payments, which can be particularly appealing if you're investing for steady cash flow or if you are closer to retirement, prioritizing income generation.
- Including bonds in your investment portfolio can help spread risk and reduce overall portfolio volatility, especially when combined with other asset classes like stocks or real estate.
- Bonds are generally considered less volatile than stocks, making them suitable for preserving capital and protecting against market downturns or economic uncertainties.
- Since they are fixed-income securities, you know exactly how much interest you'll receive and when you'll receive it, creating a level of predictability for financial planning purposes that you might not have with other investments.
- Bonds come with a number of options to manage specific risks, for example, inflation-protected securities that safeguard against inflation risk or municipal bonds that may provide tax advantages for some investors.

It's not always rosy all the time though. As you plan around these benefits, you also need to consider the possible risks you might be exposed to in the bond market. Let's explore some of them below:

- Bond prices are inversely related to interest rates, meaning that if interest rates rise, bond prices fall. This can lead to capital losses especially if you need to sell your bonds before maturity.
- Bonds may not grow at the same pace with inflation, thereby eroding the purchasing power of your investment over time, especially if the rate of inflation exceeds the bond rate.
- Investing in bonds with lower credit ratings or from issuers with uncertain financial health carries the risk of default. This means that despite the predictability of bonds, there's still a chance that you might experience a loss of principal and missed interest payments.
- While bonds offer stability and income, they generally yield lower returns compared to riskier assets like stocks over the long term. Investing too heavily in bonds may limit your potential for higher returns and wealth accumulation, while at the same time locking away your money for a long time.

Overall, a smart approach to bond investment is to balance the benefits of stability and income with the potential risks you might experience in the market. This is how you eventually build a well-rounded investment strategy that aligns with your long-term needs and objectives.

Where and How to Buy Bonds

Since you already have a brokerage account, you're one step closer to investing in bonds. How do you go about it? Where do you buy bonds? One of the most important things you need to do is conduct a thorough needs assessment. This generally means a wholesome review of your investment goals, the level of risk you are willing to take, and the time horizon within which you wish to invest.

If you're thinking short-term, you should be in the market for 1–3 years. On the other hand, if you're going long-term, you'll be in the market for more than 5 years. You could also approach the market from a medium-term angle, in which case you'll be thinking about investments around 3–5 years. This information is important because your investment time horizon determines the kind of bonds you'll put your money in, and more importantly, how you allocate your investments. Additionally, evaluate your risk tolerance to ensure your bond investments do not exceed your comfort level.

Your brokerage firm can make or break your investment strategy, especially when you consider the services they offer, and the total costs involved. Choose a brokerage firm that offers bond trading services and suits your investment needs. Look for a platform with a wide range of bond offerings, competitive pricing, and user-friendly tools for research and trading. Ensure the brokerage allows regular contributions or periodic investments if you plan to invest consistently over time.

Make the most use of your broker's research tools to explore available bonds and evaluate their features, including the issuer, credit rating, coupon rate, maturity date, and yield to maturity. Think of bonds in terms of your investment goals and time horizon. Let's say you have a long-term horizon, it might be wise to choose bonds with longer maturities and potentially higher yields.

If you've identified the bonds you want to buy, place your order through your brokerage account. Specify the quantity, price (if you are buying individual bonds), and any other relevant details. If you're planning to invest regularly over time, I'd advise you to set up automatic contributions and buy bonds at regular intervals, for example, monthly or quarterly. This approach, known as dollar-cost averaging, can help you ride out market fluctuations and build your bond portfolio gradually without paying expensively. It also takes away the risk of emotional investing.

Alternatively, you can invest in bond mutual funds or exchange-traded funds (ETFs) if you prefer a diversified approach managed by professional portfolio managers. Research bond funds in terms of their investment objectives, expense ratios, historical performance, and risk characteristics. Regular contributions to bond funds can help you accumulate shares over time and benefit from the compounding returns.

Cost and Fees

When investing in bonds, bond funds, or any other investment for that matter, you should always consider the costs and fees associated with your investments. Common costs include the following:

- Commission or Markup: Some brokerages charge a commission or markup on bond transactions. This fee may be a flat rate or a percentage of the bond's face value.
- Bid-Ask Spread: Bonds trade in the secondary market with bid and ask prices. The bid-ask spread represents the difference between the buying (ask) and selling (bid) prices. Pay attention to the spread, as it affects your transaction costs.
- Management Fees: If investing in bond funds, be aware of management fees charged by the fund provider. These fees are typically expressed as a percentage of assets under management (expense ratio).
- Redemption Fees: Some bonds or bond funds may impose redemption fees if you sell your investment before a specified holding period.

Finally, every investment you make calls for active monitoring and management. Regularly monitor your bond investments and review your portfolio's performance to make sure things are still aligned with your goals and risk tolerance. Adjust your investment strategy accordingly based on changes in market conditions, interest rates, and your financial situation. More importantly, remember the value of time. I've stressed this in all our discussions so far, that the earlier you start investing, the better. Investing in the bond market requires discipline, so make sure you stick to your plans.

Bond investments offer a valuable avenue for achieving your financial goals. By applying the principles we've discussed herein, you can navigate the complexities of bond investing confidently, building a robust portfolio that meets your objectives and plays into your long-term goal of becoming a wealthy investor. In the next chapter, we'll discuss the concept of pooled funds. We already touched on this briefly through bond funds, so you'll notice a lot of similarities as we dig deeper into the dynamics of pooled capital.

CHAPTER 7:

Funds: Understanding the Dynamics of Pooled Capital

You have the power to grow your wealth exponentially through pooled capital investments. Pooled capital is a collective effort where individuals, like yourself, come together to invest their money in various assets. This pool of capital is a unique ecosystem where your money multiplies over time, generating returns far beyond what you could achieve if you invested alone.

Pooled capital investments open doors to opportunities you might not have come across before. It's a chance to amplify your financial strength and secure your future. By pooling resources with others, you not only spread the risk but also leverage the expertise and knowledge of a diverse group of investors, and more importantly, benefit from professional management services. Whether it's investing in stocks, real estate, or venture capital, pooled capital gives you access to markets and opportunities that might have seemed out of reach if you were going it all alone.

In this chapter, we'll explore the art of investing in funds, a step-by-step guide that gives you the knowledge and tools necessary to make the most of this unique investment opportunity. We'll explore everything from the fundamentals of pooled capital to their unique characteristics, and show you how to maximize returns from your fund investments. Note that at the end of the day, fund management comes down to carefully building a growth portfolio while effectively managing risk.

Investing in Funds

A fund is essentially a pool of money collected from different investors for the purpose of investing in various assets such as stocks, bonds, commodities, or real estate. These funds are managed by professional investment managers or teams who make decisions on behalf of the investors regarding which assets to buy, sell, or hold within the fund's portfolio. There are different types of funds available to investors, including mutual funds, exchange-traded funds (ETFs), hedge funds, and pension funds, each with its own investment objectives and strategies.

Here's where the beauty of diversification comes into play. When you invest in a fund, you're not putting all your eggs in one basket. Instead, your money is spread across a range of investments. Picture it like a buffet offering different dishes. Some may perform exceptionally well while others might not do as great, but overall, your risk is spread out.

Let's say you're keen on tech companies, but you're aware that the tech industry can be volatile. Instead of investing all your money in one tech company, you could opt for a tech-focused mutual fund or ETF. This way, even if one tech company in the fund underperforms, the impact on your overall investment is cushioned by the other companies in the fund, which might be performing better or operating in different sectors altogether. Here are some reasons why you should invest in funds:

- You gain exposure to a wide array of assets like stocks, bonds, or real estate. These assets span different sectors and regions, giving you access to opportunities you might not find individually.
- Diversification helps spread risk. Since funds hold a mix of assets, poor performance from one investment won't heavily

impact your entire portfolio. This lowers the risk of significant losses.

- You have access to fund managers—experts who analyze markets and make informed decisions. They strategically allocate assets within the fund to optimize returns while managing risk. You benefit from their expertise without needing to actively manage your investments.
- With pooled resources, your funds benefit from economies of scale. Transaction costs are spread across many investors, reducing expenses. This means lower fees for you compared to managing individual investments.
- Investing in a fund is convenient. You don't need specialized knowledge or time to research individual securities. Instead, you gain diversified exposure to various markets and assets through a single investment vehicle.

Even though funds allow you the benefit of portfolio diversification, it's important to assess the fund's investment strategy, historical performance, fees, and management team to make sure that you are committing your money to a smart investment.

There are also possible downsides to investing in funds. Funds typically charge management fees and other expenses, which can reduce your overall returns. These fees are expressed as an expense ratio and are deducted from the fund's assets. While some funds have relatively low fees, others may have higher expenses, especially actively managed funds. You need to consider these fees when evaluating the potential returns of a fund you are interested in.

If you invest in multiple funds, you may encounter overlapping holdings, especially if the funds have similar investment objectives. This duplication of assets can reduce the effectiveness of diversification and increase the overall risk in your portfolio. This is why it's usually important to review the holdings of each fund carefully to make sure you're achieving adequate diversification.

Types of Funds

There are different types of funds in the market. Even though each of these funds could be ideal, the most appropriate investment comes down to your unique investment goals. What are you working towards? Why do you need to pool resources with other investors? What do you do when you achieve your investment target? These are the kind of questions you should think about as you skim through your investment options. Here are the major types of funds you'll come across in the market:

- **Mutual Funds**: Mutual funds are a pool of money from many investors that are ultimately invested in a diversified portfolio of stocks, bonds, or other securities. They are valuable because they provide diversification, professional management, and easy access to a number of markets. You can invest in mutual funds by purchasing shares directly from the fund company or through a brokerage platform. You typically need to meet the fund's minimum investment requirements.
- **Money Market Funds**: Money market funds invest in short-term, low-risk securities like Treasury bills and commercial paper. They are ideal if you are looking to add stability and liquidity to your portfolio while generating a modest level of income. They are often used for short-term cash management or as a safe haven for funds that you might wish to use in investments elsewhere.
- **Index Funds**: Index funds represent the performance of a specific market index, such as the S&P 500, which aptly covers the top 500 major companies in the US by market capitalization. Investors love them because of their low costs, broad diversification, and the ability to match market returns over the long term. Index funds usually have low expense ratios compared to actively managed funds.

- **Exchange-Traded Funds (ETFs)**: ETFs are mostly similar to mutual funds but are trade on stock exchanges just like you would trade individual stocks. They are ideal for intraday liquidity, low costs, and flexibility in trading, which makes them particularly attractive to traders. Note that there's a big difference between an investor and a trader. Traders think short-term and try to exploit price fluctuations. On the other hand, investors think long-term and are always looking for the opportunity for sustainable growth into the future. You can simply buy and sell ETF shares on the open market, and they tend to have lower expense ratios compared to mutual funds.
- **Real Estate Investment Trusts (REITs)**: REITs are entities that invest in different types of income-generating real estate assets and distribute a substantial portion of their profits to investors. They give you exposure to real estate without directly owning property and for generating consistent income through dividends. If you've ever wanted to invest in real estate but are put off by the high costs, this could be an exciting opportunity for you.
- **Hedge Funds**: Hedge funds are investment pools that use various strategies to generate returns, often with higher risk and potential for higher rewards. Their ability to hedge against market downturns and potentially outperform traditional investments makes them an ideal investment opportunity to diversify your portfolio. Note that hedge funds usually have high minimum investment requirements and are only available to accredited investors. You may need to contact the hedge fund directly or invest through a private wealth management firm.

As we mentioned earlier, each of the funds above is unique, so their benefits and possible challenges do not cut across the board. Research well enough to make sure you are putting your money in the right place, and more importantly, that your investment aligns with your long-term wealth-generation goals.

Remember the importance of investing earlier in life. By starting early, you give your investments more time to grow through the power of compounding. Every dollar you invest has the potential to earn returns, and those returns can generate even more returns over time. This compounding effect will significantly grow your wealth over the long term. Plus, the earlier you start investing, the more time you have to recover in the event of adverse market fluctuations.

Active vs. Passive Investing

One of the most important decisions you need to make as an investor is whether you'll be a passive or an active investor. Active investing refers to the strategy where you consistently buy and sell securities in an effort to achieve returns that are generally higher than those of the overall market or a designated benchmark index. In active investing, you or a professional fund manager make investment decisions based on research, analysis, and market trends. This approach often involves frequent trading and attempts to identify undervalued or overvalued assets to capitalize on short-term price movements. While active investing has the potential for higher returns, it also comes with higher costs, including management fees and transaction expenses.

If you choose active investing, here are some important pros and cons to keep in mind:

- Active investing offers the potential for higher returns compared to passive strategies. Skilled investors or fund managers aim to outperform the market by identifying undervalued assets, exploiting market inefficiencies, and timing trades effectively.

- With active investing, you have the flexibility to make decisions based on your own research, analysis, and market insights. You can actively manage your portfolio and adjust your investments in response to changing market conditions, economic trends, or individual company performance.

- As an active investor, you can take advantage of market opportunities as they arise. By actively monitoring the market, you can capitalize on short-term price movements, market dislocations, or emerging trends to potentially generate higher returns.

On the other hand, active investment comes with the following challenges:

- Active investing typically comes with higher costs compared to passive strategies. These costs include management fees, trading commissions, and other expenses associated with actively managing a portfolio. Over time, these fees can significantly erode your investment returns.
- Active investing requires a significant amount of time, effort, and expertise to research investments, analyze market trends, and monitor portfolio performance. It can be a demanding and time-consuming endeavor, especially if your resources are limited or if you do not have the required experience.
- Active investing carries a higher risk compared to passive strategies. The fact that you are attempting to outperform the market involves taking on additional risks, such as stock-specific risk, sector risk, or market timing risk. While these risks can potentially lead to higher returns, they also increase the likelihood of losses, especially if your investment decisions are based on inaccurate information or market speculation.

Passive investing takes a more hands-off approach by seeking to replicate the performance of a market index or specific asset class. Instead of trying to beat the market, passive investors try to match the returns of the chosen benchmark over the long term. Passive investing loosely represents what most people call "having your money work for you." Most passive investors have their money in index funds or ETFs that track the performance of a particular index. The S&P 500 is one such index that's widely attractive to a lot of investors. Since passive investing requires minimal trading activity and relies on the overall market's performance, it tends to have lower fees and expenses compared to active investing.

If you choose passive investing, here are some important pros and cons to keep in mind:

- Passive investing typically has lower costs compared to active investment strategies. It involves minimal trading activity and management fees. This cost-efficiency can lead to higher net returns over the long term.
- Passive investing broadly diversifies your portfolio across an entire market or asset class. By investing in index funds or ETFs that track market indices, you gain exposure to a wide range of securities, reducing individual stock risk and increasing portfolio stability.
- One thing you'll love about passive investing is its simplicity. It is a straightforward and hands-off approach to investing, such that you don't need to spend time researching individual stocks or analyzing market trends. Instead, you can invest in a few well-diversified index funds and let your investments grow over time.

On the other hand, passive investment comes with the following challenges:

- Passive investing aims to match the performance of a market index, so it may not capture the full upside potential of individual stocks or sectors that outperform the market. If you're looking for higher returns, passive investing may not be the best strategy for you.

- Passive investing lacks the opportunity to customize your investment portfolio. Since you're investing in index funds or ETFs that track predefined benchmarks, you have limited control over the specific securities held in your portfolio. This lack of customization may not align with your individual investment preferences or goals, so that's something you should strongly think about.
- Passive investing exposes you to market downturns and volatility. Since passive funds track market indices, they will reflect any declines in the underlying market. While diversification helps mitigate risk, you may still experience losses during periods of market instability.

Ultimately, the choice between active and passive investing depends on what works for you. How much time can you set aside for investment activities? If you can afford to spare time for research and other investment-related activities, active investment would be a brilliant idea for you. On the other hand, if you are unable to do that, you should consider passive investment.

This table provides a clear visual comparison of the key characteristics between active and passive investing.

Factor	**Active Investment**	**Passive Investment**
Investment Approach	Actively buying and selling securities to outperform the market or a specific benchmark	Replicating the performance of a market index or specific asset class
Investment Goal	Beat the market	Match the market
Management	Requires active management and decision-making by investors or fund managers	Requires minimal management, tracks predefined benchmarks

Factor	Active Investment	Passive Investment
Costs	Typically higher costs due to management fees, transaction expenses, and research costs	Lower costs due to minimal trading activity and management fees
Diversification	May vary based on individual investment choices and strategies	Provides broad diversification across the entire market or asset class
Risk	Higher risk due to active decision-making and potential for losses if investments underperform	Lower risk due to broad diversification and tracking market indices
Upside Potential	Potential for higher returns if investments outperform the market	Limited upside potential as investments aim to match the market
Time and Effort	Requires significant time, effort, and expertise for research, analysis, and monitoring	Requires minimal time and effort, provides a hands-off approach to investing

With this, we wrap up our discussion on the three giants of investments; stocks, bonds, and pooling capital through funds. In the next section, we will explore the new generation of investing, mostly powered by the power of modern technology, for example, cryptocurrency and Non-Fungible Tokens (NFTs).

PART III:

The New Generation of Investing

CHAPTER 8:

Investments in the World of Tech

Picture this: You're settling down on your desk, and the glow of your computer screen illuminates your face in the dimly lit room. You take a sip of your coffee, contemplating all the changes unfolding in the investment world at the moment. Technology, once a mere tool, has become the driving force behind a revolution in how investments are made, managed, and understood. From algorithmic trading to robo-advisors, the digital age has ushered in a new era of possibilities, reshaping the way you navigate the complex world of finance. How did we get here? More importantly, what can you do to get in on the action?

In this chapter, we explore insights into the new generation of investments made possible with the advancement of technology. We'll discuss the role of technology and AI in helping you make smarter investments and include popular investment trends you need to be on the lookout for if you want to make it big.

The Modern Way to Invest

Technology is all around you. It is woven seamlessly into nearly every facet, transforming the way you go about pretty much everything else in the world. From how you work to how you interact with others, technology's impact is profound. All this is possible thanks to the ease of information access. The internet serves as an expansive repository of knowledge, granting you instant access to answers, news, and research. Whether you want to learn a new skill or current events, the wealth of information available at your disposal is incredible.

Let's start with work. We're currently witnessing the influence of Artificial Intelligence (AI), not only in the workplace but everywhere else. AI is practically changing the very landscape of how tasks are accomplished. Automation and machine learning algorithms streamline processes, support efficiency, and in some cases, decision-making. Since the COVID-19 pandemic, remote working has surged in popularity, all thanks to technological advancements. Teleconferencing tools and collaboration platforms make it easier for teams to collaborate effectively from disparate locations. The flexibility afforded by remote work transforms the concept of workplace freedom, even though it often blurs the lines between professional and personal life.

Communication is another key area where you frequently experience the best of technological advancement. With the proliferation of smartphones and social media platforms, you have easy access to instant messaging, video calls, and social networking. These features not only facilitate seamless interaction, they also help you transcend geographical barriers and support the concept of building global communities. Thanks to social media and online forums you can share more vivid experiences of your personal and professional life. It's no wonder companies and major brands work so hard to create a strong social media presence. They understand that this is how people interact today, so they have to get in on the action.

There's growing interest in socially responsible investment, primarily driven by technological innovations. You can now align your financial goals with ethical considerations, supporting companies that prioritize environmental, social, and governance (ESG) factors, for example, investing in companies or brands that have a proven history of commitment to environmental conservation. It would be wise not to blindly accept what they say about their investment practices without further investigation or evidence to support their claims. This is where critical thinking, skepticism, and independent verification can help you in assessing the credibility and reliability of information or statements provided by the companies you're interested in. Instead, technology facilitates data analysis and transparency, giving you actionable information to make informed decisions on investments that reflect your desired values.

One thing you can appreciate about technology is that it has transformed the investment market, opening doors to alternative investment opportunities previously inaccessible to retail investors. Crowdfunding platforms, peer-to-peer lending, and robo-advisors offer avenues for diversification beyond conventional asset classes. These innovative investment vehicles democratize wealth creation and promote financial inclusion. Here are some investment avenues where you'll interact with the best of technology:

Financial Education Through Mobile Apps

There are lots of mobile apps that can help you understand various aspects of finance. These apps are designed to empower users with knowledge about financial concepts like budgeting, saving, investing, and managing debt. You have access to tutorials, articles, videos, and quizzes to give you more insight on these topics in a manner that's easily digestible, particularly for people who might not be savvy on investment matters.

The main advantage of such apps lies in their accessibility and user-friendly interfaces. They allow you to learn at your own pace and convenience, anytime and anywhere. Some apps also provide personalized recommendations based on your financial goals and risk tolerance. Note, however, the potential disadvantage in the quality of information provided, as not all apps provide accurate or comprehensive financial advice. Therefore, you should only use these apps as supplementary resources and seek advice from financial professionals when necessary.

Artificial Intelligence and Your Bank's Improved Customer Service

The role of AI in the banking sector is incredible. Other than streamlining traditional banking processes, banks are now leveraging the power of AI to transform customer service through chatbots and virtual assistants. These AI-powered systems can handle routine inquiries, provide account information, and offer personalized financial advice. Banks can also analyze customer data to anticipate your needs better and offer relevant products and services proactively.

AI brings much-needed convenience and efficiency to banking, reducing the amount of time you'd normally spend in the bank following up on routine or mundane tasks. You can access banking services and support 24/7 through various digital channels, including websites, mobile apps, and messaging platforms. AI-driven banking also enables faster and more accurate transactions, reducing the need for human intervention.

That being said, there will always be concerns over data privacy and security, as AI systems collect and analyze large amounts of sensitive customer information. Additionally, there are instances when you might feel your concerns would be best addressed through direct human interaction.

The Rise of Contactless Cards

When it comes to contactless cards, think of security and practicality. Contactless cards use near-field communication (NFC) technology to enable quick and secure transactions without the need to physically swipe or insert the card into a terminal. You simply tap your card on the contactless reader to complete a payment, making transactions faster and more convenient. These cards are designed to enhance security by encrypting payment information and requiring close proximity to the reader, reducing the risk of remote fraud.

The primary advantage of contactless cards is their convenience and speed. They streamline the payment process, especially for small transactions, reducing checkout times and enhancing the overall shopping experience. Contactless payments are also considered more secure than traditional magnetic stripe cards, as they generate unique transaction codes for each purchase, making them less susceptible to cloning or skimming.

It is not a fool-proof approach, however. There have been concerns about accidental or unauthorized transactions due to the proximity-based nature of NFC technology. Besides, despite its unique advantages, this approach might not yet be supported by most merchants, so there's a limited range of customers who can capitalize on its security features. If you have the opportunity to use this feature, you'll definitely appreciate the security and efficiency it brings to everyday purchases.

AI + Investments

AI has fundamentally changed the investing landscape through sophisticated tools and techniques that make it easier to analyze vast amounts of data, identify patterns, and help you make informed decisions in real-time. As far as your investments are concerned, here are some interesting ways you can tap into the power of AI:

- **Data Analysis**: You can use AI algorithms to process and analyze large datasets from various sources such as financial reports, news articles, social media, and market trends. By extracting valuable insights from this data, AI can help you identify potential investment opportunities and risks more efficiently than traditional methods.
- **Predictive Analytics**: AI-powered predictive models can forecast market trends, stock prices, and asset movements with greater accuracy. These models analyze historical data and current market conditions to anticipate future market behavior.
- **Algorithmic Trading**: AI-driven algorithmic trading systems execute trades automatically based on predefined criteria, such as price movements, volume, and market indicators. This makes it easier for you to adjust your investment portfolio aptly with respect to market changes in milliseconds, giving you an opportunity to capitalize on opportunities or mitigate risks swiftly.

- **Sentiment Analysis**: AI can analyze sentiment from news articles, social media posts, and financial reports to gauge market sentiment and investor behavior. Understanding market sentiment can help you anticipate market movements.

There are lots of AI solutions that can transform your investment journey, including AI-backed investment platforms, robo-advisors, and trading algorithms. Apart from using these solutions, the most important thing about AI is to always stay informed, as it is a largely evolving ecosystem, so try to learn as much as possible about different applications of AI, and how they play into your investment plans.

Emerging Investment Trends

Even though AI is getting all the attention in the investment space so far, there are lots of other emerging technologies that you should learn about, which act as exciting investment opportunities. Here are a few of them, which feature prominently as investment trends for the tech-savvy investor:

Fintech and Digital Assets

Fintech refers to innovative technologies that disrupt traditional financial services, such as mobile banking, peer-to-peer lending, and blockchain-based payments. Digital assets include cryptocurrencies, digital currencies, and tokenized assets.

Fintech and digital assets offer investors opportunities for diversification and exposure to disruptive technologies reshaping the financial industry. You can access new investment platforms, participate in ICOs (Initial Coin Offerings), and trade cryptocurrencies for potential high returns. However, you must also be aware of regulatory uncertainties, market volatility, and security risks associated with digital assets.

Biotech and Healthcare Innovation

Biotech and healthcare innovation involve advancements in biotechnology, pharmaceuticals, medical devices, and digital health solutions aimed at improving healthcare outcomes and patient care.

This is a brilliant opportunity for investment exposure to cutting-edge medical treatments, therapies, and technologies with the potential for significant returns. If you go this route, pay attention to regulatory approvals, clinical trial outcomes, and competitive dynamics when evaluating investment opportunities in this sector.

Infrastructure and Clean Energy

Infrastructure and clean energy investments focus on sustainable infrastructure development, renewable energy projects, and green technologies aimed at reducing carbon emissions and addressing climate change.

The prospect of stable returns, government incentives, and long-term growth prospects are attractive incentives for investments in this sector. Renewable energy projects, such as solar and wind farms, offer predictable cash flows and potential tax benefits. Your due diligence should include assessing regulatory policies, project risks, and market demand.

Insurtech

Insurtech refers to technology-driven innovations in the insurance industry, including digital insurance platforms, usage-based insurance, and AI-powered underwriting and claims processing.

Insurtech investments are an opportunity to capitalize on the digital transformation in the insurance industry, improve operational efficiency, and enhance customer experiences. Startups disrupting traditional insurance models generally offer the potential for high returns, but you must still research well before investing, especially on competition, regulation, and technological risks.

Quantum Computing

Quantum computing harnesses the principles of quantum mechanics to perform complex computations exponentially faster than classical computers, unlocking new possibilities in cryptography, optimization, and scientific research.

The excitement in this venture centers around exposure to groundbreaking technological advancements with the potential to revolutionize various industries. Even though quantum computing startups and research initiatives present opportunities for significant returns, you should be aware of their unique technical challenges, scalability issues, and long-term development timelines.

Metaverse

Widely touted as the next phase in the evolution of the internet, the metaverse is a collective virtual space created by the convergence of virtual reality (VR), augmented reality (AR), and the internet, where users interact with digital environments and each other in real-time.

There are lots of investment opportunities in the metaverse, including virtual real estate, digital assets, gaming, entertainment, and e-commerce within immersive virtual worlds. Metaverse investments are an exciting blend of innovation and creativity, with potential for high growth and innovation. However, it is a largely developing space, so you should research well to understand the dynamics of technological adoption, user engagement, and applicable regulatory aspects when evaluating investment opportunities in the metaverse.

Robo-Advisors

Robo-advisors are digital platforms that use algorithms and automation to construct and manage investment portfolios based on your financial goals. They typically offer a range of diversified investment options, including ETFs and mutual funds, tailored to your unique investor profile. They assess your risk preferences through online questionnaires or behavioral analysis and recommend suitable asset allocations. They can also rebalance your portfolio periodically to maintain your desired risk-return profile and optimize investment performance.

Robo-advisors operate on a digital platform with minimal human intervention, making it easier to offer investment management services at lower fees compared to traditional human advisors. This cost-efficiency appeals to a lot of investors, especially if you're looking for affordable and accessible investment solutions.

Most robo-advisors offer additional financial planning tools and educational resources to help you set and achieve your financial goals. These tools may include retirement planning calculators, tax optimization strategies, and goal-tracking features.

Robo-advisors have experienced rapid growth in recent years, driven by the growing demand for low-cost, automated investment solutions among retail investors. The convenience, accessibility, and transparency appeals to a broad spectrum of investors, particularly millennials and Gen Z. For this reason, the use of robo-advisors has expanded beyond retail investors to serve institutional clients, financial advisors, and retirement plan investors. The institutional adoption of robo-advisory platforms for portfolio management and client servicing has also contributed to the overall growth and credibility of the industry.

Despite their effectiveness, robo-advisors are not a replacement for human investment managers. Instead, you should think of them as an efficient support system, complementing the role of your investment manager. Robo-advisors and human investment managers can coexist and complement each other in investment management. While robo-advisors excel in providing cost-effective, rule-based portfolio management services for tech-savvy and cost-conscious investors, human advisors offer personalized financial advice, behavioral coaching, and holistic wealth management services. There will always be moments when the best help comes from your manager, especially in situations that require in-depth context analysis.

Some financial advisory firms have adopted hybrid models that combine robo-advisory technology with human advisory services to offer a blended approach to investment management. This hybrid model allows you the benefit of the convenience and efficiency of robo-advisors without compromising on the personalized advice and guidance from your investment manager.

Micro-Investing

Micro-investing refers to the practice of investing small amounts of money regularly, typically through mobile apps or online platforms, into financial investments like stocks, ETFs, or cryptocurrencies. The goal of micro-investing is to make investing accessible to individuals with limited capital and encourage long-term saving and wealth accumulation. To this end, micro-investing platforms allow you to start investing with minimal capital, usually with no minimum investment requirement. This accessibility lowers the barrier to entry for new investors, particularly younger generations and those with limited disposable income.

Most of the micro-investing apps have automated features, such as round-up contributions or recurring deposits, which make it easier to invest small amounts of money regularly without having to actively manage your investment. This automation encourages consistent saving and investing habits over time. You also have the option of purchasing fractional shares of stocks or ETFs, so you can own a small portion of high-priced assets that you may not be able to afford at full price. This feature enables greater diversification and access to a broader range of investment opportunities.

One thing you'll love about micro-investing platforms is that most of them have educational resources, tutorials, and investment insights to help you learn about investing basics, financial literacy, and investment strategies. These resources are quite empowering, as they help you build confidence in your investment journey.

The ease of getting into investment aside, you should also be aware of the following possible challenges in micro-investing:

- Micro-investing platforms may have a limited selection of investment options compared to traditional brokerage accounts, restricting your ability to customize your portfolio.

- While micro-investing platforms usually have low or no account minimums, they may charge fees for transactions, account maintenance, or premium features, which can eat into your investment returns, especially for small balances.
- The ease of micro-investing and automated features may tempt you to overtrade or make impulsive decisions, which can lead to unnecessary fees and poor investment performance.
- Automated investing features may not accommodate your personal preferences or investment strategies, limiting your control over your portfolio and some investment decisions.

What I can tell you about micro-investing, robo-advisors and other emerging investment strategies is to use them as a complementary approach to your overall investment strategy. This is a smart way to diversify your approach, instead of putting all your eggs in one basket, especially when you're just getting started.

Finally, the beauty of technology is that it's constantly evolving. This means that even the approaches and solutions we've discussed herein might be outdated at some point in the future. Your challenge, therefore, is to stay updated on emerging trends in the wider investment ecosystem and identify solutions that can support your overall investment objective. In the next chapter, we'll delve into the dynamics of cryptocurrency, a controversial but noteworthy investment opportunity you must pay attention to.

CHAPTER 9:

Cryptocurrency: A Deep Dive into the Decentralized Future

The buzz around cryptocurrency has been going on for years. Perhaps there's a slim chance you might not know much about cryptocurrency, or crypto as it's often referred to, but you do know about Bitcoin, right? Bitcoin has taken the world by storm and usually features in conversations about the next stage in the evolution of money. We've come from the days of barter trade to paper currency and coins, online money transfers, and now Bitcoin. Despite its popularity and market share, Bitcoin is just one of thousands of cryptocurrencies you'll come across.

So, back to the excitement about cryptocurrency—it's everywhere, right? People are talking about it at work, on social media, even at family meetings. It's like the hottest topic when it comes to investing. And why wouldn't it be? The potential for massive returns is just too tempting to ignore.

Everywhere you turn, there's news of someone striking it rich with Bitcoin or Ethereum, or some other cryptocurrency. It's the modern-day gold rush, with everyone scrambling to get in on the action. The idea of a decentralized currency, free from government control, is captivating. And let's not forget about all those success stories—the early adopters who invested peanuts and are now living the high life.

But here's the thing: Is crypto just a passing fad, like Tamagotchis? Or is it the real deal, a groundbreaking investment opportunity that's here to stay? Sure, the volatility can be ridiculous at times, and the market is still largely unregulated. But could that be part of the allure? After all, higher levels of risk in an investment often correlate with the potential for greater rewards or returns. While taking on more risk can lead to higher possibility of success or profitability, it's important to note that such outcomes are not always guaranteed, hence the need for you to carefully weigh the risks and rewards before investing in the crypto market.

So, what do you think? Is crypto the future of investing, or are we all just caught up in a speculative frenzy that's bound to come crashing down? It's a question worth thinking about as you navigate the exciting and sometimes perilous world of cryptocurrency.

Blockchain 101

Think of blockchain as a digital ledger, a record-keeping system that's decentralized and transparent. Instead of one central authority controlling everything, like a bank or the government, blockchain operates on a network of computers called nodes. These nodes work together to verify and record transactions in a secure and immutable (cannot be changed) way.

When you make a transaction with cryptocurrency, whether it's buying, selling, or transferring coins, that transaction gets bundled together with other transactions into a "block." Each block contains a unique cryptographic hash, which acts as a digital fingerprint. Once a block is created, it's added to the existing chain of blocks, forming a chronological and unalterable record of all transactions, hence the name "blockchain."

Now, here's where it gets interesting. Because blockchain is decentralized and distributed across thousands of nodes, it's incredibly secure. To tamper with a transaction, you'd have to change the entire chain of blocks on every single node simultaneously, which is virtually impossible. This makes blockchain resistant to fraud, hacking, or any kind of manipulation.

Blockchain is the underlying technology that makes cryptocurrency possible in the first place. Without blockchain, there would be no way to securely and transparently record transactions in a peer-to-peer digital currency system. In essence, blockchain is the backbone of cryptocurrency, providing the trust and reliability that traditional financial systems lack.

Cryptocurrency

Cryptocurrency is basically digital money. Unlike other forms of money; however, it is decentralized. That means there's no single bank or government controlling it all. All cryptocurrency transactions are recorded on the blockchain. However, this information is not recorded in one place. It's duplicated and stored on thousands of computers all over the world, as we've seen in the blockchain concept above.

A new cryptocurrency is made through a process known as mining. Mining means using highly advanced and powerful machines to solve complex math problems, and when the miners crack the code, they're rewarded with new cryptocurrency. Most cryptocurrencies have a limit on how much of their supply can ever exist. This inherently deals with the possible problem of flooding the market with cryptocurrencies. It's not like governments print money whenever they feel like it. This scarcity goes a long way in determining the cryptocurrency's value over time, just like with precious metals.

Now, when you want to send cryptocurrency to someone, you use a wallet. Crypto wallets are like your own personal bank account, but more secure. You have a public address where people can send you money, and a private key that acts like a super-secret password to access your funds, that no one else can access.

There are several factors that could affect the value of cryptocurrencies. These are as follows:

- **Supply and Demand**: Like any other asset, the value of cryptocurrencies is influenced by supply and demand dynamics. Limited supply, coupled with increasing demand, tends to drive up prices, while excessive supply or reduced demand can lead to price declines.
- **Market Sentiment**: Cryptocurrency markets are highly sensitive to investor sentiment, which can be influenced by news, regulatory developments, technological advancements, and market speculation. Positive news or developments often lead to increased investor confidence and higher prices, while negative news can trigger sell-offs and price drops.
- **Technological Innovations**: The underlying technology of a cryptocurrency can significantly impact its value. Upgrades, improvements, or innovations in blockchain technology can enhance a cryptocurrency's utility, security, and scalability, leading to increased adoption and value.
- **Regulatory Environment**: Regulatory decisions and policies adopted by governments and regulatory bodies can have a significant impact on cryptocurrency markets. Favorable regulations or legal clarity can boost investor confidence and adoption, while restrictive regulations or bans can dampen market sentiment and reduce demand. For example, the recent approval of Bitcoin Spot ETFs spurred a lot of activity in the market, with major players in the financial sector like BlackRock and Fidelity making major moves, much to the amazement of their customers and stakeholders.
- **Market Liquidity**: The liquidity of a cryptocurrency, which refers to the ease of buying or selling it without significantly impacting its price, also affects its value. Cryptocurrencies with higher liquidity tend to be more stable and attractive to investors.

It's worth noting that cryptocurrency is a vastly evolving ecosystem so far, so you should always be on the lookout for news and new developments in the wider blockchain divide. Knowledge of these factors can help you navigate the complex and volatile world of cryptocurrencies and make smarter investment decisions.

Decentralized Finance

Decentralized finance, commonly known as DeFi, is a financial system where transactions and other financial activities take place without the need for traditional intermediaries like banks or financial institutions. In DeFi, you have direct control over your assets, and transactions are executed through smart contracts on blockchain networks like Ethereum. Instead of relying on centralized entities to facilitate transactions, DeFi platforms use decentralized protocols, allowing for greater transparency, accessibility, and autonomy in financial operations.

Fiat Money

Fiat money refers to traditional currencies issued by governments, for example, the U.S. Dollar, Euro, or Japanese Yen. Unlike cryptocurrencies, which are decentralized and based on blockchain technology, fiat money gains its value from the trust and confidence we have in the issuing government and its economy. Essentially, the value of fiat money is backed by the government's authority and the stability of its economy, as well as the belief that others will accept it as a medium of exchange, unit of account, and store of value.

The Giants of Cryptocurrency

There are lots of cryptocurrencies in the market at the moment, probably thousands, and there will be many more in the future as the sector continues to evolve. Here's a brief overview of five of the top cryptocurrencies in the market at the moment. You can use this as a reference point for any other crypto asset you're considering for the future.

Bitcoin (BTC)

Bitcoin operates on a decentralized blockchain network, utilizing a proof-of-work consensus mechanism. It enables peer-to-peer transactions without the need for intermediaries. There will only be a limited supply (21 million coins) of Bitcoin. Bitcoin is widely seen as a digital gold and a hedge against inflation. You can, therefore, buy and hold Bitcoin as a long-term store of value or as part of a diversified portfolio.

On top of that, you can also look forward to its high liquidity. The fact that it is widely accepted globally makes Bitcoin a good asset in your investment portfolio, particularly buoyed by its massively established network. Bitcoin also enjoys a first-mover advantage in the market. It's widely recognized as a store of value and has strong security through decentralization.

On the flip side, you'll always have to worry about scalability issues, relatively slow transaction speeds, and high energy consumption due to the proof-of-work consensus mechanism.

Ethereum (ETH)

Ethereum is a decentralized platform that enables smart contracts and decentralized applications (DApps) to be built and run without downtime, fraud, or interference from third parties. Some of its standout features include smart contract functionality, a large developer community, and the ability to create tokens and DApps.

Ethereum's flexibility makes it an ideal platform for developers, with massive potential for innovation in various industries. Ethereum is often considered a platform for decentralized finance (DeFi) and other blockchain applications. Investors buy Ether to participate in initial coin offerings (ICOs), stake in Ethereum 2.0, or invest in promising DApps and projects built on the Ethereum network.

That being said, Ethereum has struggled with scalability issues over the years, mostly because of the growing number of users and projects hosted within its ecosystem. There's also the challenge of security vulnerabilities in smart contracts and regulatory uncertainty for DApps.

Binance Coin (BNB)

Binance Coin is the native cryptocurrency of the Binance exchange, one of the largest cryptocurrency exchanges globally. It is a utility token for trading fee discounts, token sales, payments, and staking on the Binance Smart Chain and other activities in the wider Binance ecosystem.

BNB enjoys strong utility within the Binance ecosystem, hence its widespread adoption. There are occasional token burns to reduce supply and counter the prospect of inflation. The good news is that you can buy BNB to benefit from discounted trading fees on Binance, participate in token sales on the platform, and potentially benefit from the growth of the Binance ecosystem.

One notable problem with BNB is its dependency on the success of the Binance exchange. This makes it a centralized project, essentially contravening the very concept of blockchain computing.

Cardano (ADA)

Cardano is a blockchain platform that provides a more secure and scalable infrastructure for the development of smart contracts and DApps. Its core features include a peer-reviewed research-driven approach, layered architecture for scalability and security, potential for interoperability, and a focus on sustainability.

You could buy ADA to support the development of the Cardano ecosystem, participate in staking, and potentially benefit from the adoption of Cardano-based DApps and projects in the future.

Unfortunately, development progress has been slow over the years, and looking at the prospect of competition from other smart contract platforms, scalability remains unproven.

Solana (SOL)

Solana is a high-performance blockchain platform designed for decentralized applications and crypto-currencies. Its standout features include a high throughput (65,000 transactions per second), low transaction fees, and fast confirmation times. Recent developments in its infrastructure include a potential upgrade from 65,000 to a million transactions per second.

Solana thrives on the backbone of a strong community of developers, scalability, high throughput, and low fees, which continue to attract investors and developers alike to the platform. You can buy SOL to participate in the Solana ecosystem, stake in network validation, and invest in projects and DApps built on the Solana blockchain.

Investing in cryptocurrencies comes with unique risks due to their volatility and regulatory uncertainties. You should always conduct thorough research and consider factors like the project's fundamentals, the team of developers behind the project, technology, adoption, and market trends before making investment decisions.

Mining for Digital Gold

Cryptocurrency mining is the process of validating and adding transactions to a blockchain ledger using computational power. Mining is usually frowned upon because of its high energy consumption, especially in proof of work (PoW) systems like Bitcoin and Ethereum.

In Bitcoin mining, miners compete to solve cryptographic puzzles using specialized hardware called ASICs (Application-Specific Integrated Circuits). These puzzles require massive computational power and consume substantial amounts of electricity. As Bitcoin mining difficulty increases, so does the energy consumption associated with it.

Ethereum switched from PoW to proof of stake (PoS) in 2022, with Ethereum 2.0. In proof of stake, validators are chosen to create and validate new blocks based on the number of coins they hold and are willing to "stake" as collateral. This method requires significantly less energy compared to proof of work, as it eliminates the need for resource-intensive mining computations.

We can summarize the difference between the two consensus mechanisms as follows:

Proof of Work (PoW)

- It requires miners to solve complex mathematical puzzles.
- It is energy-intensive, as miners compete to find the correct solution.
- It incentivizes miners with newly minted coins and transaction fees.
- It provides security through computational work, but requires significant energy consumption.

Proof of Stake (PoS)

- Validators are chosen to create and validate new blocks based on the coins they hold and are willing to stake.
- It's energy-efficient, as it doesn't rely on computational work.
- Validators are incentivized by earning transaction fees and newly minted coins.
- It's generally considered more environmentally friendly than proof of work.
- It's adopted or planned by several cryptocurrencies, including Ethereum 2.0.

While both proof of work and proof of stake have their pros and cons, proof of stake is generally considered more environmentally friendly due to its lower energy consumption. Ethereum's transition to proof of stake with Ethereum 2.0 could address concerns about energy usage and environmental impact associated with mining.

Investing in Your First Crypto

The first thing you need to figure out when it comes to crypto investing is the exchange you'll use. Choose a reputable cryptocurrency exchange platform where you can buy, sell, and trade cryptocurrencies. Research different exchanges to find one that suits your needs in terms of security, fees, supported cryptocurrencies, and user experience. Sign up for an account on your chosen exchange. You'll likely need to verify your identity by providing personal information and sometimes submitting identity documents, depending on the exchange's regulations.

Deposit funds into your exchange account using a bank transfer, credit card, or other accepted payment methods, and you'll be ready to trade in whichever cryptocurrency you want. Always conduct thorough research on each cryptocurrency, considering factors like its technology, use case, team, and market trends. Once you've decided on a cryptocurrency, place your buy order on the exchange. Specify the amount you want to purchase and confirm the transaction.

Crypto Storage

After purchasing cryptocurrencies, you'll need to store them securely to protect your investment. You can choose between hard wallets (hardware wallets) and soft wallets (software wallets) for storage.

Buy a hardware wallet device from a reputable manufacturer. Popular options include Ledger Nano S, Ledger Nano X, and Trezor. Follow the instructions provided by the manufacturer to set up your hardware wallet. This typically involves initializing the device, setting a PIN code, and generating a recovery seed phrase. After that, use the wallet's interface or compatible software to transfer your cryptocurrencies from the exchange to your hardware wallet address.

The good thing about hard wallets is that they have a high level of security as private keys are stored offline, protecting your investment against hacking and malware. Besides, you also enjoy support for a wide range of cryptocurrencies.

On the other hand, hardware wallets are quite expensive. The costs are usually prohibitive for many users. There's also the risk of physical damage or loss of the device.

For soft wallets, choose between any reputable software wallet provider and download their wallet application onto your computer or mobile device. Examples include Exodus, Electrum, and MyEtherWallet. After that, follow the prompts to create a new wallet within the software. This usually involves generating a private key and backup seed phrase.

Once everything is set up, you can now send your cryptocurrencies from the exchange to your software wallet address using the wallet receiving address.

Soft wallets are convenient and accessible, usually free to use, and easy to set up and use across multiple devices. On the flip side, they tend to be more susceptible to hacking and malware compared to hard wallets, if not properly secured. The other challenge with soft wallets is that they are overly reliant on the native security measures of the device and operating system.

Ultimately, even though both hard wallets and soft wallets provide secure storage options for cryptocurrencies, each comes with its own set of pros and cons that you should be aware of. Ideally, you should choose the storage solution that best meets your needs when investing in cryptocurrencies.

Minimizing the Risks in Digital Currencies

Every investment comes with some level of risk. Even inherently secure investments like government bonds usually have a risk potential, even though it might be quite minimal. Here are some of the common risks that you'll need to plan around when investing in digital currencies:

- Digital currencies like Bitcoin and Ethereum are known for their extreme price volatility. The value of cryptocurrencies can fluctuate significantly over short periods, leading to potential gains but also substantial losses.
- Regulatory frameworks surrounding cryptocurrencies vary widely across countries and jurisdictions. In some cases, they are non-existent at all. Where they exist, changes in regulations or government actions can influence the legality, taxation, and use of cryptocurrencies, leading to uncertainty for investors and users.
- Digital currencies are susceptible to cybersecurity risks, including hacking, phishing attacks, and malware. Exchanges, wallets, and other cryptocurrency platforms are always targeted by cybercriminals, hence the risk of theft of funds or personal information.
- Unlike traditional financial systems, digital currencies often lack consumer protections such as deposit insurance or recourse for fraudulent transactions. Once a cryptocurrency transaction is completed, it is irreversible, and there is no central authority to intervene in disputes.
- Cryptocurrency markets are relatively unregulated compared to traditional financial markets, making them susceptible to manipulation and fraud. Pump-and-dump schemes, insider trading, and market manipulation tactics can artificially inflate or deflate cryptocurrency prices, leading to losses if you make investment decisions based on such flawed information.

Risks in Cryptocurrency

The risks we've mentioned above apply to cryptocurrency and digital assets in general. This means that whether you're investing in Bitcoin or any other blockchain project for that matter, these risks will always be imminent. Let's now look at the risks that apply to cryptocurrency, particularly when used as a form of payment:

- Cryptocurrency prices can fluctuate rapidly, making it harder to determine the value of goods or services priced in cryptocurrency. This volatility can lead to uncertainty for both buyers and sellers.
- Cryptocurrency transactions may incur significant fees during periods of network congestion or high demand. These fees can vary depending on the cryptocurrency used and the transaction size, potentially making small transactions uneconomical.
- Cryptocurrency transactions are irreversible once confirmed on the blockchain. If a transaction is sent to the wrong address or disputed, there is no recourse to reverse the transaction or recover the funds.

Looking at the possible risks above, there are two possible scenarios that you might consider as far as building wealth using cryptocurrency is concerned. Are you approaching cryptocurrency for speculative purposes or as an investment? Let me explain this:

Speculating in cryptocurrencies means buying and selling digital assets with the aim of profiting from short-term price movements. As a speculator, you depend on market trends, technical analysis, and sentiment to make trading decisions, instead of fundamental analysis.

Investing in cryptocurrencies means buying digital assets with the expectation of long-term growth and value appreciation. You will typically conduct research on the fundamentals of cryptocurrencies, such as technology, adoption, and use cases, before making investment decisions.

The difference between these two is that speculation carries a higher risk than investment because it involves short-term trading and can be influenced by market sentiment and speculation rather than underlying value. Investments, on the other hand, are based on a belief in the underlying value of the cryptocurrency and its potential for future adoption and utility.

Your choice, therefore, should come down to your investment goals. Once again, I'll ask you the simple question—what are you working towards? From your answer, you can then decide whether or how the crypto approach you choose aligns with your long-term vision, and make the right choice.

Ultimately, even though digital currencies come with lots of opportunities for innovation and financial inclusion, they also come with unique risks. Knowledge of these risks can help you adopt appropriate risk management strategies to protect your investment.

Finally, building on our knowledge of digital currencies, let's shift our focus to another exciting development in the blockchain ecosystem, Non-Fungible Tokens (NFTs). In the next chapter, we'll delve into what NFTs are, how they work, and the opportunities and challenges they present in the evolving landscape of digital assets.

CHAPTER 10:

NFT: Into the World of Digital Art and Tokenized Assets

NFTs have become both a catalyst and a controversial topic in modern art. They usher you into a digital gallery where traditional boundaries between art and technology get blurred over time. It's quite the revolution, to be honest, and modern technology is right at the heart of it. If you're an art enthusiast, you find yourself immersed in a dynamic fusion of creativity and blockchain technology. NFTs offer artists a new canvas, making it easier for them to digitize their work and authenticate its uniqueness through blockchain, thus challenging conventional notions of ownership and value. This also takes away the brokerage aspect of art, where third parties have often profited off the work of artists, taking commissions for their agency role. Through NFTs, artists now have direct access to their customers, audiences, and global markets.

Yet, as you delve deeper into the world of NFTs and modern art, you encounter a series of debates and contradictions. Proponents argue that NFTs democratize the world of art, allowing artists to bypass traditional gatekeepers and directly engage with a global audience. They emphasize the potential for artists to gain greater control over their talent and monetize their work in ways previously not directly possible.

The intersection of NFTs and modern art raises fundamental questions about authenticity and the essence of art itself. As you contemplate the value of a digital token representing ownership of a piece of art, you grapple with the intangible nature of NFTs compared to the tangible experience of traditional artwork. Yet, amidst these uncertainties, there's an undeniable allure to the potential of NFTs to redefine how we create, consume, and perceive art in the digital age. Whether NFTs represent a fleeting trend or a transformative shift in the world of art remains to be seen, but their influence on modern art is undeniable, prompting reflection and reevaluation of the age-old concept of art.

The Money in Digital Art

NFT stands for non-fungible token. Now, what does that mean? Well, think of it like this: "non-fungible" means it's unique, one of a kind, unlike something that's interchangeable like money. And "token" refers to the digital certificate that proves ownership or authenticity.

Let's say you have a digital painting or a video clip. Anyone can download a copy of it, right? But with an NFT, you can prove that you own the original. It's like having a digital certificate of authenticity that says, "Hey, this digital item is mine, and I can prove it using blockchain technology."

NFTs are often used in the world of digital art, music, videos, and even virtual real estate. People buy and sell them just like physical assets, except it's all happening in the digital space. It's a way for creators to monetize their work and for collectors to own digital assets in a way that's verifiable and unique.

NFTs have stirred up some controversy too. While some people argue that it's just a hype bubble waiting to burst, others see it as a revolutionary way to redefine ownership in the digital age. Whatever your take is, one thing we know for sure is that NFTs are shaking up the way we think about digital ownership.

How did this all happen? I mean, we didn't have NFTs before, right?

The concept of NFTs emerged around 2012 with the creation of the Colored Coins project on the Bitcoin blockchain. This project aimed to represent real-world assets on the blockchain by "coloring" specific bitcoins to differentiate them from others, thus creating a form of digital ownership.

But it wasn't until 2017 that the modern NFT movement really took off with the launch of CryptoKitties. These were unique digital cats that could be bought, sold, and bred on the Ethereum blockchain. Each CryptoKitty was represented by an NFT, making it one of the earliest mainstream use cases for non-fungible tokens. As CryptoKitties gained popularity, artists and creators began to explore the potential of NFTs for digital art and collectibles. Platforms like SuperRare and Rarible emerged, allowing artists to tokenize their work and sell it directly to collectors, all backed by blockchain technology.

In 2021, the NFT market went mainstream, riding off the wave of creatives stuck in their homes thanks to the COVID-19 lockdowns. High-profile sales were making headlines around the world. From digital art selling for millions of dollars to sports highlights and tweets being tokenized, NFTs became a hot topic of conversation and controversy, and the fact that most of the world was isolated in their homes made it even easier, because most people practically had nothing to do.

Today, NFTs continue to evolve, with new use cases emerging across various industries and debates raging about their environmental impact, market speculation, and the future of digital ownership. It's been a whirlwind journey from the early days of experimental projects to the vibrant and sometimes chaotic ecosystem we see today.

How NFTs Work

NFTs work by using blockchain technology to create unique digital tokens that represent ownership of an asset. These tokens can be used to represent anything from digital art to music to virtual real estate. When you purchase an NFT, you are not actually buying the underlying asset itself. Instead, you are buying a token that is associated with the asset. You're essentially purchasing ownership of this digital asset and acquiring the associated token. This ownership is recorded on the blockchain, which is a decentralized ledger that keeps track of all transactions, and provides proof of authenticity and ownership.

The blockchain ensures that NFTs are unique and cannot be replicated. This makes them a valuable way to represent ownership of digital assets. So, how does this uniqueness work? Well, NFTs contain metadata that defines their specific characteristics, such as their owner, the creator, and any other relevant information. This metadata is what distinguishes one NFT from another and gives it its value.

Here is a simplified overview of how NFTs work:

1. An artist creates a digital asset, such as a piece of art or a music track.
2. The artist "mints" the asset by creating an NFT that represents it.
3. The NFT is stored on the blockchain.
4. The artist can then sell the NFT to a collector.
5. The collector can then use the NFT to prove ownership of the digital asset.

Now, one of the cool things about NFTs is their programmability. Smart contracts, which are self-executing contracts with the terms of the agreement directly written into code, can be used to automate certain actions related to NFTs. For example, a smart contract can ensure that a percentage of future sales of an NFT goes back to the original creator, providing them with ongoing royalties. In a nutshell, NFTs work by leveraging blockchain technology to create unique digital assets that can be bought, sold, and owned with a high degree of transparency and security.

Here's something you should always remember: Unlike cryptocurrencies like Bitcoin or Ethereum, which are fungible (meaning one unit is interchangeable with another), NFTs are non-fungible, meaning each one is distinct and cannot be replicated or exchanged on a one-to-one basis.

Value in NFTs

These digital assets exist online. Anyone can easily print a copy. How then, do they become valuable? Well, while it's true that you can print a copy of your favorite painting and hang it in your living room, the fact is that what you have is just a copy. That's where NFTs shine. There will only ever be one original item, identifiable by its metadata—that's one smart way to take the fight to online piracy!

The value of an NFT often comes from its uniqueness, meaning each one is distinct and irreplaceable. We can attribute this uniqueness, or inherent value to the following factors:

- Scarcity: Limited edition or one-of-a-kind NFTs tend to hold more value because there's a finite supply. Just like rare physical collectibles, scarcity drives up demand.
- Creator: The reputation and popularity of the creator can significantly influence the value of an NFT. If a well-known artist or celebrity is associated with the NFT, it can attract more attention and value.
- Provenance: The history and authenticity of the NFT can impact its value. Buyers are often interested in knowing the origin of the NFT and whether it's been verified by the creator or a reputable source.
- Utility: Some NFTs come with additional benefits or access rights, such as exclusive content, virtual experiences, or membership privileges. These added utilities can increase the perceived value of the NFT.
- Cultural significance: NFTs that capture significant moments, trends, or cultural phenomena may hold value due to their historical or social importance. For example, an NFT representing a viral meme or a landmark event in the digital world could become valuable as a piece of internet history.

- Market demand: Ultimately, the value of an NFT is also influenced by market demand. If there are buyers willing to pay a premium for a particular NFT, its value will increase accordingly.

One thing I'd like to remind you is that NFT values can be subjective and fluctuate based on various factors, for example trends, market sentiment, broader economic conditions, or even a tweet by Elon Musk! What one person finds valuable in an NFT might not be the same for someone else. Ultimately, it's a combination of factors that determine the worth of an NFT in the eyes of collectors and enthusiasts.

Investing in NFTs

NFTs are an exciting investment opportunity beyond the traditional stocks or real estate. NFTs represent a unique opportunity in the digital age. Here are some reasons why you might want to consider investing in NFTs:

- **Diversification**: NFTs in your investment strategy are a unique opportunity to diversify your portfolio. While traditional investments like stocks and bonds have their place, adding NFTs introduces a new asset class with potentially different risk-return profiles. By spreading your investments across various asset types, you can better mitigate the overall risk of your portfolio. The distinct characteristics and market dynamics around NFTs can provide a hedge against volatility in other sectors, thereby enhancing the resilience of your portfolio.
- **Potential for High Returns**: Although investing in NFTs carries risks like any other asset class, the potential for high returns cannot be overlooked. Some NFTs have demonstrated extraordinary appreciation in value over relatively short periods. By carefully selecting NFTs backed by strong communities, renowned creators, or unique features, investors can position

themselves to capitalize on significant value appreciation. While past performance is not indicative of future results, the rapidly evolving nature of the NFT market presents opportunities for savvy investors to generate substantial returns on their investments.

- **Participation in Emerging Markets**: Investing in NFTs allows you to participate in an exciting and rapidly evolving market in the early stages of development. As blockchain technology continues to gain momentum, the NFT market is poised for significant growth and innovation. By getting involved now, you have the opportunity to shape the direction of this emerging market and position yourself at the forefront of a transformative trend in digital ownership and commerce. Imagine the people who invested in Bitcoin in the early days when it was worth less than a dollar. At the point of this publication, a single Bitcoin was worth at least $69,000.
- **Supporting Artists and Creators**: Beyond financial returns, investing in NFTs enables you to support artists and creators directly. By purchasing their work as NFTs, you give them a platform to monetize their creations and gain recognition for their talent and creativity. This direct relationship between creators and investors is necessary for a vibrant ecosystem where artistic expression is valued, incentivized, and rewarded, thereby fueling further innovation and cultural enrichment.
- **Liquidity and Accessibility**: NFTs offer unparalleled liquidity and accessibility compared to traditional assets. With trading platforms and marketplaces facilitating transactions 24/7 on a global scale, you can buy, sell, and trade NFTs with ease. This liquidity gives you ample room to enter and exit positions as needed, allowing for greater flexibility and portfolio management. Additionally, the accessibility of NFTs democratizes investment opportunities, opening up investment

markets to individuals from diverse backgrounds and geographic locations.

- **Innovation and Technology**: Investing in NFTs is not just about acquiring assets; it's also about embracing innovation and technology. NFTs leverage blockchain technology to authenticate ownership, ensure scarcity, and enable seamless transactions in a decentralized manner. By investing in NFTs, you're not only positioning yourself to potentially profit from market trends but also contributing to the ongoing development and adoption of cutting-edge technologies that have the potential to reshape various industries. As blockchain technology continues to evolve and mature, the possibilities for NFTs are virtually limitless, making them an intriguing investment opportunity.

The Cons

Before investing in NFTs, you should also think of the possible challenges you might experience in this market. Consider this as due diligence, just like you would conduct for any other investment opportunity for that matter. Here are some concerns you should be aware of as you get into the NFT market:

- **Volatility**: The NFT market's volatility can be staggering, with prices experiencing rapid and sometimes unpredictable fluctuations. Factors such as changing trends, shifts in investor sentiment, and sudden bursts of speculation can lead to significant price swings over short periods. This volatility can pose challenges for investors, as it increases the risk of sudden losses and requires a high tolerance for market turbulence. Without careful risk management strategies in place, you may find yourself exposed to substantial financial risks in a highly volatile market.

- **Speculative Investment**: Investing in NFTs inherently involves speculation, as the value of digital assets is often based on subjective factors like perceived scarcity, cultural relevance, and future demand. Unlike traditional financial assets with underlying economic fundamentals, the value proposition of NFTs can be unpredictable, making it difficult to assess their long-term investment potential accurately. With this in mind, you must be prepared for the possibility of substantial fluctuations in prices and exercise caution when making investment decisions based on speculative factors alone.

- **Lack of Regulation**: The NFT market operates with minimal regulatory oversight compared to traditional financial markets, leaving you vulnerable to various risks, for example, fraud, scams, and market manipulation. The absence of clear regulatory frameworks and standards for NFTs can create opportunities for criminals to exploit unsuspecting investors through deceptive practices like fake listings, plagiarized content, and pump-and-dump schemes. Without robust regulatory safeguards in place, it's up to you to exercise due diligence and skepticism in your investment.

- **Subjectivity of Value**: Determining the value of NFTs is inherently subjective and often based on intangible factors such as artistic merit, cultural significance, and perceived scarcity. Unlike traditional financial assets with quantifiable metrics and fundamentals, the value of NFTs can vary widely depending on individual preferences, tastes, and market dynamics. This subjectivity introduces uncertainty and complexity into the investment process, as you have to rely on personal judgment and market sentiment to assess the potential value of NFT assets accurately.

Minting NFTs

Minting NFTs means that you are creating and registering a unique digital asset on a blockchain network. When you mint an NFT, you're essentially encoding ownership and authenticity information into a digital token, which is then stored securely on the blockchain. This process establishes a verifiable record of ownership and ensures the scarcity and uniqueness of the digital asset.

To mint an NFT, you typically use a specialized platform or marketplace designed for NFT creation and distribution. These platforms guide you through the process, allowing you to upload the digital file you want to tokenize, specify metadata such as title, description, and attributes, and configure any additional settings such as royalties or unlockable content.

Once you've completed the minting process, the NFT is assigned a unique identifier, often referred to as a token ID, and is recorded on the blockchain, making it immutable and publicly accessible. This enables anyone to verify the ownership and authenticity of the NFT by referencing its blockchain record.

Minting NFTs can be an exciting way to showcase your creativity, share your work with a global audience, and potentially monetize your digital assets. Whether you're an artist, content creator, or collector, minting NFTs offers a novel opportunity to participate in the burgeoning digital economy and contribute to the growing ecosystem of blockchain-based assets.

Buying and Selling NFTs

There are lots of options you can consider if you want to buy or sell NFTs. Marketplaces like OpenSea, Rarible, and Foundation provide a wide range of NFTs across different categories, from which you can browse listings, place bids, and make purchases directly from the comfort of your home. Next, come up with a budget and investment strategy tailored to your financial profile. Decide how much capital you're willing to allocate to NFT investments and whether you prefer to focus on specific categories or diversify across multiple types of

NFTs. Consider factors like the reputation of creators, the rarity of assets, and the potential for long-term value appreciation.

You can also explore cryptocurrency exchanges that have integrated NFT trading capabilities. Platforms like Binance and Coinbase usually have NFT marketplaces where you can buy, sell, and trade NFTs alongside cryptocurrencies. These exchanges provide a familiar interface for users already active in the cryptocurrency space, making it convenient to diversify your portfolio with NFT investments.

You could also come across random opportunities to buy and sell NFTs directly from artists, creators, and collectors through their social media platforms, online forums, or dedicated communities on Discord and Telegram. This option is a more personal and direct approach to acquiring NFTs while directly supporting the creators behind them.

Regardless of where you choose to buy and sell NFTs, you must always conduct thorough research, consider the timing, market conditions, and pricing strategies, verify the authenticity of listings, and exercise caution when transacting in digital marketplaces.

Finally, remember to manage risk by diversifying your NFT portfolio, staying vigilant to avoid scams and fraudulent activity, and only investing what you can afford to lose. With careful research and planning NFTs can be a rewarding investment opportunity to participate in the digital economy and potentially generate significant returns over time.

PART IV:

Investments and the Future You

CHAPTER 11:

Investing in the You of the Future Through Retirement Funds

Retirement isn’t something many young people think about, yet you should. You might think you're too young to worry about it, but here's the thing—the earlier you start, the better off you'll be in the long run. Sure, retirement might seem so many years away, something your parents or grandparents deal with, but time flies. Before you know it, those years will sneak up on you, and wouldn't it be nice to have a comfortable retirement fund waiting when you retire?

Imagine this: you have the power to shape your future, starting right now. The sooner you begin investing in your retirement, the more time your money has to grow and work for you. It's like planting a seed and watching it turn into a flourishing tree over time.

Think of it as an adventure that includes exploring the world of investing, and learning about stocks, bonds, and other financial investments that can help you achieve financial independence in the future. So, why wait? Embrace the curiosity and urgency to secure your financial future. Remember, it's never too early to start planning for tomorrow—and the journey begins now!

Never Too Young to Invest for Retirement

Retirement, from a financial point of view, represents a critical juncture in your life where the fruits of your labor meet your aspirations for a comfortable, stress-free future. It's the culmination of years of hard work, discipline, and financial planning. Think of retirement as the ultimate reward for your dedication, a time when you can finally enjoy the fruits of years of toil without the constraints of waiting for a regular paycheck to be able to handle your expenses.

However, retirement isn't just a distant dream; it's a tangible goal that requires careful consideration and proactive planning. It's about ensuring that you have enough financial resources to maintain your desired lifestyle once you stop working. This means having a steady stream of income to cover your living expenses, healthcare costs, and any unforeseen emergencies that may arise.

Every dollar you contribute to your retirement accounts has the potential to grow over time, thanks to the power of compounding interest. By starting early and consistently contributing to your retirement savings, you're setting yourself up for long-term financial success. Besides, investing in your retirement offers you the opportunity to take advantage of various tax incentives and employer-sponsored plans, such as 401(k)s or IRAs. These vehicles allow you to save and invest your money in a tax-efficient manner, maximizing your returns and minimizing your tax liabilities over time.

One of the most important lessons I like to share with my mentees about retirement is the need to recognize that the earlier you start investing in your retirement, the more time your money has to grow and work for you. Even small contributions made early on can have a significant impact on your overall financial security in retirement, making it easier to cater to your needs in your later years.

Ultimately, investing in your retirement isn't just about securing your financial future; it's about ensuring your peace of mind and freedom to live life on your terms. It's about having the flexibility to pursue your passions, travel the world, or simply relax and enjoy your well-deserved leisure time.

Start Right Away

Instead of thinking about investing as a financial activity, consider it a powerful tool that can help you achieve your retirement goals and enjoy financial security in the future. By investing wisely and consistently, you can build a robust portfolio that provides for your needs and desires during retirement.

First and foremost, investing offers you flexibility and freedom to enjoy retirement life on your terms. It's about creating options and opportunities for yourself, so you can live the life you've always dreamed of once you retire. Whether it's traveling the world, pursuing your passions, or simply enjoying quality time with loved ones, investing gives you the financial independence to make those choices without worrying about money.

One crucial reason not to delay planning for retirement is that waiting too long can make it harder to start. Time is your greatest asset when it comes to investing, and the earlier you begin, the better off you'll be. Starting early allows you to take advantage of compounding interest, which means your money has more time to grow and multiply exponentially.

Furthermore, don't fall into the trap of thinking that marriage is a safety net for your retirement. I've seen a lot of young women make this mistake, so it's quite apt to call you out on it, in case you've been thinking along the same line. While sharing financial responsibilities with a spouse can provide some security, it's essential to have your own retirement savings and investments. Relying solely on a partner's income or retirement savings can leave you vulnerable in the event of divorce, illness, or other unforeseen circumstances.

Remember, you're working towards living a long life! With advancements in healthcare and technology, people are living longer than ever before. This means your retirement could last decades, and you'll need substantial savings to support yourself during those years. Investing early ensures that you have the financial resources to enjoy a comfortable and fulfilling retirement lifestyle. Even small amounts can earn interest and add up over time, so you don't need a huge sum of money to start investing for retirement. By making regular contributions, no matter how small, you can harness the power of compounding and watch your savings grow steadily over the years.

Finally, statistically speaking, you probably won't work full-time between now and your retirement day. Life is unpredictable, and there may be periods of unemployment, career changes, or other challenges along the way. Investing in your retirement today provides a safety net during such times and ensures that you have a source of income to rely on when you're no longer working. So, don't wait another day—start planning and investing for your future now. Your retirement dreams are within your reach, and it's never too early to start working toward them.

The Value of Social Security

Social Security is a government program established in the United States to provide financial support to retired individuals, as well as those with disabilities and successors of deceased workers. It operates by collecting payroll taxes from current workers and using those funds to pay benefits to eligible recipients. While Social Security serves as a crucial safety net for many Americans, relying solely on it for retirement income is not advisable for several reasons.

Firstly, Social Security benefits are intended to supplement retirement income, not serve as the primary source. The average monthly benefit payment is modest, often providing only a fraction of the income needed to maintain a comfortable standard of living in retirement. So if you've been thinking of retiring on Social Security benefits, you need to rethink that plan.

The future of Social Security is uncertain due to demographic shifts and economic challenges. As the population ages and the ratio of retirees to workers increases, the strain on the Social Security system grows. Additionally, factors such as longer life expectancy and lower birth rates contribute to the financial pressures facing the program. Without significant reforms, there's a possibility that Social Security benefits may be reduced in the future or eligibility requirements may change, making it less reliable as a sole source of retirement income.

Another reason to not rely solely on Social Security is that benefit levels may not keep up with the pace of inflation. While Social Security benefits are adjusted annually based on the Consumer Price Index (CPI), the increases may not fully offset rising living expenses for retirees. This means that over time, the purchasing power of Social Security benefits could diminish, making it challenging to cover your essential expenses in retirement.

Furthermore, Social Security benefits are based on your earnings history and the age at which you choose to claim them. For individuals with higher incomes, Social Security benefits may represent only a small portion of their pre-retirement earnings. Depending solely on these benefits may result in a significant drop in income during retirement, leading to financial strain and forcing you to make uncomfortable lifestyle adjustments.

Thus, even though Social Security provides important financial support for retirees, it should not be something you solely rely upon as your sole source of retirement income. To ensure a secure and comfortable retirement, you should supplement your Social Security benefits with personal savings, investments, employer-sponsored retirement plans, and any other source of income. This diversity in your retirement portfolio makes it easier to mitigate risk and be better prepared for uncertainties in the future.

Factors Shaping Your Retirement Needs and Savings Strategies

Given what you now know about Social Security, we go a step further and explore important factors that could influence the amount of money you need for retirement, and more importantly, whether you can meet your retirement goals or not.

- Lifestyle Expectations: Your desired lifestyle in retirement significantly influences how much money you need to save. Factors such as travel, hobbies, entertainment, and healthcare costs can vary widely and should be considered when setting your retirement savings goals.

- Inflation: The purchasing power of money decreases over time due to inflation. Therefore, it's essential to account for inflation when estimating your retirement expenses and determining how much you need to save.
- Life Expectancy: Longer life expectancies mean that as a retiree, you may need to save more to sustain your lifestyle over an extended period. You should consider your family history, health status, and access to healthcare when estimating your life expectancy. This is an important part of planning, because the last thing you want is to impose your financial needs on your loved ones once you retire, yet they also have their own needs to take care of.
- Healthcare Costs: Healthcare expenses tend to increase with age, making it essential to budget for medical care, prescription drugs, long-term care, and other healthcare-related expenses in retirement.
- Investment Returns: The returns you earn on retirement savings investments play a significant role in determining how much you need to save. Higher returns may allow for lower savings contributions, while lower returns may necessitate higher savings rates to meet your retirement needs and goals.
- Retirement Age: You might not have thought about this before, but I'll ask it anyway. When do you wish to retire from active employment? The age at which you retire will influence your retirement savings plan. Retiring earlier may require larger savings to fund a more extended retirement period, while delaying retirement can allow for more time to save and potentially higher Social Security benefits.
- Debt and Financial Obligations: If you carry a lot of debt into retirement, for example, mortgages, car loans, or credit card debt, you may need to allocate more of your retirement income

towards debt repayment. The solution here is to try and minimize debt before retirement as much as possible.

- Employer-Sponsored Retirement Plans: Participation in employer-sponsored retirement plans, such as 401(k) will always affect your retirement savings plan. This is because your employer matches your contributions and investment options, helping you grow your retirement savings over time.

Finally, you should always have an emergency plan in place. Unexpected expenses or financial commitments can disrupt your retirement plan if you never set up adequate savings to mitigate such instances. Speaking of contingency plans, you should make a point to regularly review your retirement plans and adjust accordingly from time to time, as your circumstances in life change. This is a smart way to better estimate your retirement savings needs and take proactive steps to meet your financial goals as they evolve over time.

Social Security Benefits and Your Retirement Goals

When evaluating how your Social Security benefits can contribute to or limit progress toward meeting your retirement savings goal, there are several factors that come into play. You should always consider the amount of your projected Social Security benefits. The Social Security Administration provides estimates of your future benefits based on your earnings history and projected retirement age. Understanding how much you can expect to receive from Social Security can help you gauge how much additional retirement savings you'll need to accumulate.

If you've worked consistently and earned a decent income throughout your career, your projected Social Security benefits can contribute significantly to your retirement income. These benefits could serve as a reliable source of income to cover basic living expenses in retirement, potentially reducing the amount you need to withdraw from your retirement savings.

However, you must also understand the limitations of your Social Security benefits. The average monthly benefit payment is modest, and for many retirees, it may not be sufficient to maintain their lifestyle without additional sources of income. If you rely solely on Social Security for retirement income, you may find yourself facing financial constraints or needing to make significant lifestyle adjustments.

Besides, Social Security benefits may be subject to taxation, depending on your total income in retirement. If you have other sources of income, such as retirement account withdrawals or investment earnings, a portion of your Social Security benefits could be taxed, further reducing their cushioning impact on your overall retirement income.

Therefore, it's safe to say that even though Social Security benefits can contribute to your retirement income and help alleviate some financial pressure, they may not be sufficient to cover all your expenses. To enjoy a comfortable and financially secure retirement, you need to supplement Social Security with personal savings, investments, and other sources of income. This is why you should be thinking about how you can secure the bag, today!

How to Start Investing in Your Retirement

When planning for your retirement, understanding the different types of retirement accounts available can help you make informed decisions that align with your investment goals. Let's explore four important retirement accounts you should consider investing your money in.

Roth IRA

Roth IRAs offer tax-free withdrawals in retirement, as your contributions are made with after-tax dollars. Additionally, Roth IRAs have no required minimum distributions (RMDs) during your lifetime, allowing your investments to grow tax-free for as long as you like. Roth IRAs also provide flexibility, allowing you to withdraw your contributions (but not earnings) penalty-free at any time. This investment is ideal if you expect your tax rate to be higher in retirement than it is currently. You might also want to consider it in case you are looking for flexibility in retirement withdrawals and prefer tax-free growth on your investments.

Traditional IRA

Traditional IRAs offer tax-deferred growth, meaning your contributions are tax-deductible in the year they are made, and your investments grow tax-free until withdrawal in retirement. Additionally, Traditional IRAs provide a potential tax break during your working years, as contributions may lower your taxable income. You should consider this investment if you expect to be in a lower tax bracket once you retire than during your working years. The Traditional IRA is also ideal if you want immediate tax benefits on your contributions.

401(k)

401(k) plans are employer-sponsored retirement accounts that offer tax-deferred growth similar to Traditional IRAs. One significant advantage of 401(k)s is your employer matching your contributions, which provides free money to boost your retirement savings. Additionally, 401(k) plans often offer a wide range of investment options and higher contribution limits compared to IRAs. This plan is also suitable for you if you are looking for higher contribution limits and diversified investment options.

Pensions

Pensions provide guaranteed income in retirement, usually based on years of service and salary history with your employer. Unlike other retirement accounts, pensions offer a fixed monthly benefit for life, providing an element of financial security and stability in retirement. Pensions are ideal for you if you have access to employer-sponsored pension plans and look forward to guaranteed income once you retire. They are particularly a good option if you want predictable cash flow and peace of mind in retirement.

To figure out which of these retirement accounts aligns best with your investment goals, think about your current tax situation, expected future tax rates, whether you have access to employer-sponsored plans or not, and the kind of flexibility you need to access your money when you retire.

Let's now briefly explore simple steps to guide you on how to invest in the accounts we've discussed:

Investment Guide: Roth IRA

- **Step 1: Eligibility**—To contribute to a Roth IRA, you must have earned income (such as wages or self-employment income) within the year and meet specific income limits set by the IRS. Check the current income thresholds to ensure eligibility.
- **Step 2: Choose a Provider**—Select a financial institution or brokerage firm that offers Roth IRA accounts. Consider factors such as fees, investment options, customer service, and online platform usability when choosing a provider.
- **Step 3: Open an Account**—Complete the application process to open a Roth IRA account with your chosen provider. You'll need to provide personal information, such as your Social Security number, date of birth, and contact details.
- **Step 4: Fund Your Account**—Make contributions to your Roth IRA account. You can contribute up to the annual contribution limit set by the IRS, which may vary based on your age and income. Take advantage of the opportunity to contribute the maximum amount allowed each year to maximize your retirement savings.
- **Step 5: Invest Your Contributions**—Allocate your contributions into investment options offered by your Roth IRA provider. Consider diversifying your investments across various asset classes, such as stocks, bonds, mutual funds, or

exchange-traded funds (ETFs), to manage risk and optimize returns over time.

Smart investment tip: Given the tax-free growth and flexibility of Roth IRAs, I'd encourage you to invest in assets with high growth potential, for example, stocks or equity-based funds. Hold onto these investments for the long term so you can benefit from compound growth and avoid early withdrawal penalties.

Investment Guide: Traditional IRA

- **Step 1: Eligibility**—Ensure you meet the eligibility requirements for contributing to a Traditional IRA, including having earned income and being below certain income thresholds if you're covered by an employer-sponsored retirement plan.
- **Step 2: Select a Provider**—Choose a financial institution or brokerage firm that offers Traditional IRA accounts. Look at their fees, investment options, customer service, and any other factor that could make your investment process easier when reviewing your options.
- **Step 3: Open an Account**—Just like the Roth IRA, complete the application process to open a Traditional IRA account with your chosen provider. Avail all the necessary personal information and agree to the terms and conditions of the account.
- **Step 4: Contribute to Your Account**—Contribute to your Traditional IRA account, up to the annual contribution limit set by the IRS. Take advantage of the potential tax deduction for contributions, which can lower your taxable income for the year. Finally, allocate your contributions to various investment options available from your Traditional IRA provider. Weigh your options against your risk tolerance, investment objectives,

and time horizon when selecting investments for your portfolio.

Smart investment tip: To get the most value from your Traditional IRA, contribute the maximum amount allowed each year and consider potential tax deductions for those contributions. Put your money in tax-efficient assets like index funds or tax-exempt bonds, to reduce your taxable income while at the same time maximizing your growth potential.

Investment Guide: 401(k)

- **Step 1: Enroll in Your Employer's Plan**—If your employer offers a 401(k) plan, enroll in the plan by completing the necessary paperwork or online enrollment process. Review the plan documents and investment options available to participants.
- **Step 2: Contribution Amount**—Decide how much you want to contribute to your 401(k) account each payment period. Try to contribute at least enough to take full advantage of any employer-matching contributions offered, as this is essentially free money.
- **Step 3: Investment Options**—Choose from the investment options available within your employer's 401(k) plan. Factors like risk, return potential, and diversification will affect the value of your investment portfolio.
- **Step 4: Automatic Contributions**—Schedule automatic contributions to your 401(k) account through payroll deductions. Automating contributions ensures consistent savings and helps you avoid the temptation to spend the money elsewhere.
- **Step 5: Review and Readjust Regularly**—Monitor the performance of your 401(k) investments regularly and adjust

your asset allocation with respect to the changes in your life. Rebalance your portfolio from time to time to maintain your desired risk level and investment objectives.

Smart investment tip: Always take full advantage of your employer-matching contributions by contributing enough to your 401(k) account to receive the maximum match offered by your employer. For the best outcome, invest in a diversified mix of low-cost index funds or target-date funds to simplify portfolio management and achieve long-term growth.

Investment Guide: Pension

- **Step 1: Understand Your Employer's Pension Plan**—Find out as much as possible about your employer's pension plan, including eligibility requirements, vesting schedule, and benefit calculation formula. Review the plan documents provided by your employer or human resources department to figure out whether it fits into your retirement vision.

- **Step 2: Determine Your Benefit**—Calculate your estimated pension benefit based on your years of service, salary history, and other factors specified in the pension plan. Use online calculators or consult with your employer's benefits department for assistance.

- **Step 3: Plan for Supplemental Savings**—While pensions provide a valuable source of retirement income, consider supplementing your pension benefits with additional retirement savings through other accounts, such as IRAs or employer-sponsored retirement plans.

- **Step 4: Ensure Vesting Requirements**—Understand the vesting schedule of your employer's pension plan, which determines when you become entitled to receive pension benefits. Ensure you meet the vesting requirements to qualify for pension benefits upon retirement.

- **Step 5: Coordinate with Other Retirement Accounts**—Coordinate your pension benefits with other retirement accounts, for example, your IRAs or 401(k)s, to optimize your overall retirement income strategy. Things like tax implications, withdrawal timing, and asset allocation should come to mind when integrating pension benefits with other sources of retirement income.

Smart investment tip: The best way to get the most value from pension benefits is to maximize your years of service with your employer, so you can increase your pension benefit amount. Where possible, stay with your employer long-term to maximize benefits from their pension fund, and ensure financial security in retirement.

You've learned about the importance of investing in your future through retirement funds like Roth IRAs, Traditional IRAs, 401(k)s, and pension fund accounts. Each opportunity we've discussed comes with unique benefits and challenges that can significantly affect your retirement savings goals. Remember that the ultimate goal is to take proactive steps toward securing your financial future.

Let's now shift our attention to investing in yourself today, where we'll explore the power of personal development to increase your earning potential and pave the way toward financial independence. By investing in yourself today, you'll not only enhance your career prospects but also lay the foundation for a more prosperous and fulfilling life.

CHAPTER 12:

Investing in the You Now

The best investment you'll ever make is in yourself. Forget about the stocks, bonds, and retirement accounts for a moment. If you don't invest in yourself, you might not have the capacity to realize and benefit from the gains of your investments. Thus, you need to see yourself as someone worthy of a good life, and put in the work to achieve it.

Investing in yourself by acquiring knowledge and honing skills initiates a transformative journey that extends far beyond personal growth. It begins with your own development, broadening your perspectives, enhancing critical thinking abilities, and fostering adaptability. With this growth, you have the confidence and resilience to overcome challenges and pursue your aspirations relentlessly.

Beyond professional success, self-investment plays an important role in your financial well-being. Your knowledge and skills serve as invaluable assets in generating income, building wealth, and making informed investment decisions. You are better equipped to secure better-paying jobs, start successful businesses, and achieve financial stability and prosperity. Come to think of it, investing in yourself also means investing in your physical and mental well-being. You can achieve this with knowledge about nutrition, exercise, stress management, and mental health, leading to a healthier lifestyle and better overall well-being.

The positive ripple effect of self-investment extends to your interpersonal relationships and community impact. An empowered woman is one of the most powerful forces in this world. Improved self-awareness and communication skills strengthen your relationships, making it easier to collaborate with other people, and resolve conflicts effectively. By sharing your expertise, mentoring other women, and contributing to collective growth and development, you help to build stronger and more resilient communities. Ultimately, investing in you today means prioritizing your self-growth and leaving behind a legacy of accomplishment and inspiration.

You Are Your Best Investment

Investing in yourself is the cornerstone of financial success for women today. Why? Because, unlike other investments, the returns from investing in yourself are lifelong and resilient, no matter the economic climate. Consider your knowledge and skills. They're your personal assets that no recession or market crash can devalue. Whether you're advancing your education, learning new skills, or honing existing ones, every bit of knowledge you acquire stays with you and can be leveraged for opportunities in any economic situation.

Equally important is your personality and attitude. Your mindset can either propel you forward or hold you back financially. Cultivating a positive attitude, resilience, and a growth mindset can empower you to overcome obstacles, seize opportunities, and confidently navigate financial challenges.

Then there's the issue of networking. Your ability to connect with others can significantly influence your financial trajectory. Building and nurturing relationships opens doors to opportunities, collaborations, mentorship, and even funding. A robust network can get you some invaluable support, guidance, and access to resources that will be useful in your journey to financial success.

In essence, I'd encourage you to think of it this way—when you invest in yourself, you're not only enhancing your skills and knowledge but also building your mindset and expanding your network. These are all essential aspects for achieving financial prosperity. So, prioritize yourself, because in doing so, you're investing in the most reliable asset you'll ever have: yourself!

If you're looking to build a financially secure future, here are some important areas where you should pay the most attention:

- **Financial Literacy**: Learn budgeting, saving, investing, and debt management. Explore different investment vehicles, for example, stocks, bonds, mutual funds, and real estate. This is important because financial literacy is the foundation of making sound financial decisions and building wealth over time.
- **Marketable Skills**: Identify skills that are in demand in your industry or desired career path. I'd encourage you to go beyond your industry and learn skills in core areas, for example, digital marketing, coding, data analysis, project management, and communication. These are marketable skills that increase your earning potential and make you more valuable in the job market or as an entrepreneur.
- **Entrepreneurship**: Take time to learn the basics of starting and running a business, including business planning, marketing, sales, and financial management. Understand how to research and identify market needs, develop products or services, and create value for customers. Entrepreneurship offers the potential for unlimited income and allows you to have greater control over your financial future.
- **Emotional Intelligence**: Emotional intelligence is one of those skills that many people lack in society today, yet it's one of the most valuable, not just in your financial journey, but in life as well. Develop self-awareness, self-regulation, empathy, and interpersonal skills. This means learning how to manage stress, handle setbacks, and build strong relationships. Emotional intelligence is crucial for success in both personal and professional life, and will influence decision-making, communication, and collaboration.

- **Communication Skills**: Work on your verbal and written communication skills, including public speaking, negotiation, and persuasion. Learn how to effectively convey ideas, articulate your value, and build rapport with others. Strong communication skills enhance your ability to influence others, negotiate better deals, and advance your career.
- **Networking**: Develop networking skills to build and maintain professional relationships. This means networking effectively both online and offline, including leveraging social media platforms and attending industry events where necessary. Nothing opens doors to opportunities for you like your networks. It will also facilitate your career growth, and give you easy access to mentors, collaborators, and potential clients or investors.
- **Continuous Learning**: Get in the habit of learning. Make it a lifelong experience, so you can be updated on industry trends, technological advancements, and market developments. There's lots of useful material out there, from books to online courses, workshops, and seminars. The goal here is to be able to recognize and adapt to changes, stay relevant in your field, and remain competitive in the job market or as an entrepreneur.

These are important tips I've picked up over the years from my mentors, and have been valuable in my life. If you can focus on developing these areas and acquiring the associated skills and knowledge, you can significantly increase your chances of achieving financial independence and building a secure future for yourself.

How to Invest in Yourself

Investing in yourself is crucial for your personal growth and success. The question is to get there. One of the most important lessons I tell women I interact with all the time is that you need peace of mind above everything else. Without peace of mind, things will hardly ever fall into place. This is why you need to prioritize your mental health.

Without a sound mind, achieving your goals becomes significantly more challenging. Make self-care a priority, whether it's through meditation, therapy, or simply taking time for yourself each day, do it. In a world that's so unfair, rough, and unkind to women, your mind is your safe haven, so protect it by all means.

Declutter your physical and mental space to reduce stress, improve focus, and create room for new opportunities and experiences. Let go of anything that no longer serves you, whether it's material possessions, negative thoughts, or toxic relationships. Here are some other valuable tips on how to invest in yourself:

- Set clear, achievable goals that align with your values and aspirations. These goals will serve as your roadmap, guiding you toward your desired destination. Break them down into smaller, manageable steps to make them less daunting and more attainable.

- Seek out a mentor who can offer guidance, support, and valuable insights based on their own experiences. A mentor can provide invaluable advice, help you navigate challenges, and accelerate your growth and learning curve.

- If you've never done so, start journaling today. It's such a simple habit, but it goes a long way in tracking your progress, helping you reflect on your experiences, and clarifying your thoughts and feelings. Writing can be a powerful tool for self-discovery and personal development.

- Practice gratitude regularly to cultivate a positive mindset and appreciate the blessings in your life. Gratitude can help shift your focus from what you lack to what you have, fostering a greater sense of contentment and fulfillment. Gratitude can help you embrace an abundance mindset, ushering in one of the most powerful and transformative experiences in your life.

- Identify and break any bad habits that are holding you back from reaching your full potential. Whether it's procrastination, negative self-talk, or unhealthy lifestyle choices, commit to replacing these habits with positive ones that align with your goals and values.
- Get organized to create a sense of clarity, efficiency, and productivity in your life. Develop systems and routines that help you manage your time, tasks, and resources effectively.
- Procrastinate less by setting deadlines, breaking tasks into smaller chunks, and eliminating distractions. Practice self-discipline and focus on taking consistent action toward your goals, even when you don't feel like it.
- Create a budget to manage your finances responsibly and ensure that you're investing in your future financial well-being. Track your income and expenses, prioritize your spending, and set aside savings for emergencies and long-term goals.

These points barely scratch the surface of what it takes to invest in yourself. I'm sure you'll come across more points over time. I can, however, summarize these points in four key areas, which have been valuable points of growth in my life, and could also be valuable pillars in your life—invest in your relationships, career, health, and your money.

Investing in healthy relationships means nurturing the very foundation on which your life evolves. Your relationships will always influence every move you make, hence the need to cultivate strong bonds with friends, family, mentors, and colleagues. This not only enriches your life with love and support but also opens doors to opportunities you might never have encountered alone. These relationships can provide valuable guidance, connections, and emotional sustenance as you navigate the ups and downs of your journey toward financial independence.

Next, every step you take to invest in your professional growth—whether it's acquiring new skills, seeking out challenging projects, or expanding your network—lays another brick in your journey to success. Your career is not merely a means to an end but an opportunity for personal fulfillment and financial stability. By dedicating time and effort to nurturing it, you're laying the groundwork for future prosperity.

Pay attention to your finances. Save diligently, budget wisely, and make informed decisions about your investments and expenditure. Cultivate financial literacy and keep looking for growth opportunities, whether through entrepreneurship, investing, or passive income streams.

Finally, invest in your health. Your body and mind are the most precious assets you own, and protecting them is essential for achieving your long-term goals. Prioritize self-care, exercise, proper nutrition, and mental well-being to ensure you have the energy, focus, and resilience needed to pursue your ambitions. Remember, good health is the bedrock upon which all other achievements are built.

Protecting Your Investments with Insurance

Insurance is a contract between yourself (the policyholder) and an insurance company, wherein the insurer agrees to provide financial protection or reimbursement against specified losses or damages in exchange for the payment of premiums. In simpler terms, insurance is a risk management tool that helps you or your business hedge against potential financial losses from unforeseen events like accidents, natural disasters, illness, or death.

Insurance is, therefore, a safety net for your finances, protecting you against unexpected events that could otherwise leave you in financial ruin. When you invest in insurance, you're essentially transferring the risk of certain losses to an insurance company in exchange for a premium.

Imagine you've just bought a new car. You're excited about hitting the road, but there's always that lingering worry about what would happen if you were in an accident. Here's where insurance comes in. By purchasing auto insurance, you're ensuring that if your car gets damaged or you're involved in a collision, the insurance company will help cover the costs of repairs or medical bills, depending on the coverage you have.

Similarly, when you buy a home, you want to protect it against unforeseen events like fires, natural disasters, or theft. Homeowners insurance provides that protection, giving you peace of mind knowing that if something happens to your home, you won't have to bear the full financial burden alone.

Now, insurance isn't just about protecting your assets; it can also be an investment in itself. Certain types of insurance, like whole life or universal life insurance, not only provide coverage but also accumulate cash value over time. This means that as you pay your premiums, a portion of that money goes into a savings or investment account within the policy. Over the years, this cash value grows, and you can use it as a source of funds for things like retirement, education expenses, or emergencies.

Types of Insurance Policies

Since there are different types of insurance policies, varied according to each insurer, let's narrow our focus to those that are relevant to your investments:

Life Insurance

These include term life insurance, whole life insurance, and universal life insurance. Before you sign up, try and understand the coverage amount based on your financial obligations and goals. Compare quotes from different insurance companies to find the best policy for your needs.

Fill out an application with personal and medical information, then schedule a medical exam according to the insurer's guidelines or provide medical records for assessment. Review and sign the policy documents once approved.

Health Insurance

In this category, you'll find individual health insurance, employer-sponsored health insurance, and government-sponsored health insurance (e.g., Medicare, Medicaid). To sign up, first assess your healthcare needs and budget and then research available plans from insurance providers or your employer.

Compare the coverage plans, premiums, deductibles, and copayments. Complete the application form with your personal information and that of your dependents. Provide any required documentation, such as proof of income or citizenship. Review the policy terms and conditions before finalizing the contract.

Property Insurance

Here you have homeowners insurance, renters insurance, and landlord insurance. First, make sure you evaluate the value of your property and belongings. I'd advise you to get professional appraisers for this, so you insure the true value of your property. During the assessment, discuss the level of coverage needed for risks like fire, theft, or natural disasters.

Since you're trying to get the best value for your money, obtain and compare quotes from different insurance companies that deal in property insurance. Complete the application form with property details and your desired coverage. Schedule an inspection if required by the insurer. If everything checks out, review and sign the policy documents upon approval.

Auto Insurance

Common types of auto insurance include liability insurance, collision insurance, and comprehensive insurance. Some of the important factors you should consider when applying for this cover include your driving habits, vehicle value, and state requirements. Ask for quotes from multiple insurers according to your coverage needs.

You'll need to provide personal information, vehicle details, and driving history on the application form, then choose the coverage levels and deductibles that fit your budget. Review the policy terms, including coverage limits and exclusions, then sign the policy documents upon acceptance.

One thing you should always remember about insurance is that it is a legally binding and enforceable contract, so it's important to read and understand the fine print. If possible, have an insurance professional, financial advisor, or attorney go over the documents with you, to make sure it is in your best interests according to the laws in your jurisdiction. A lot of people have had the unfortunate experience of suffering a loss for which they believed they were insured, only to realize that their insurance contract was void, so they were not compensated at all. When applying for any type of insurance, it's essential to be honest and accurate in providing information, as inaccurate information could lead to claim denials or policy cancellations later on.

So, if you're using insurance to look out for your investments as a valuable investment opportunity, the bottom line is that insurance gives you financial security and stability in a world filled with uncertainties. It's a smart way to protect what matters most to you and build a stronger financial future.

Evaluating Your Current Progress

Whatever you are working on, you need to regularly evaluate and track your progress. This is necessary for any investment, whether it involves financial resources or personal development. These assessments provide valuable insights into the effectiveness of your strategies, allowing you to make informed decisions and adjustments along the way. By gauging current progress and identifying opportunities for improvement, you can stay on course toward your goals, maximize efficiency, and optimize possible outcomes.

Without ongoing evaluation and tracking, you risk stagnation, missed opportunities, and setbacks in your journey. Therefore, you need to establish a habit of regular assessments to ensure that you're making meaningful progress and continuously working towards improvement. This process is important for several reasons, but we'll highlight four of the most important ones:

1. **Accountability**: Regularly tracking your progress holds you accountable for your actions and commitments. When you have clear metrics and milestones to measure against, you're more likely to stay accountable to yourself and others involved in your investment journey. Knowing that you'll need to report on your progress can help keep you focused and disciplined.
2. **Motivation**: Tracking progress provides tangible evidence of your efforts paying off, which can keep you motivated to continue moving forward. Seeing incremental improvements or milestones can act as positive reinforcement, which goes a long way in boosting your morale and fueling your determination to achieve your goals.
3. **Continuous Improvement**: By tracking progress, you can identify areas where you're excelling and areas that may need improvement. This feedback loop allows you to adjust your strategies, tactics, or behaviors where necessary. Whether it's refining your investment approach or honing your skills, regular assessment and adjustment facilitate ongoing growth and improvement.
4. **Prioritization**: Progress tracking helps you prioritize your efforts and resources effectively. By assessing what's working well and what's not, you can allocate your time, energy, and resources to activities that have the most significant impact on your investment outcomes. This ensures that you focus your efforts on tasks that move you closer to your goals while minimizing distractions or inefficiencies.

Whether you're working towards financial growth or personal development, you should always track your progress as you pursue your goals. This is an opportunity to make adjustments as needed, increasing your chances of success and achieving your objectives more efficiently. Here are some steps you can follow and track your progress:

Step 1: Assess Your Current Financial Situation

Start by taking stock of your current financial status. Collect information on your income, expenses, savings, investments, and debts. This will give you a clear picture of where you stand financially.

Journal Entry: Write down your income sources, monthly expenses, savings, investments, and outstanding debts. Include any assets you own, such as property or vehicles, as well as any liabilities. This journal will serve as a baseline for tracking your progress over time.

Step 2: Set Clear Investment Goals

Define investment goals that align with your age, level of risk you are comfortable with, time horizon, and desired lifestyle. Whether it's saving for retirement, buying a home, or funding your children's education, having specific goals will guide your investment strategy.

Journal Entry: Write down clear and achievable goals, whether it's saving for retirement, buying a home, or funding your children's education. Be sure to include both short-term and long-term objectives, along with target deadlines for each goal.

Step 3: Track Your Progress Regularly

Come up with a system to track your investment progress regularly. This could involve setting up spreadsheets or using financial tracking apps. Monitor the performance of your investments against your goals and adjust your strategy accordingly.

Journal Entry: Your tracking system should include metrics such as investment returns, portfolio diversification, and savings growth. Schedule regular check-ins with yourself to review your progress and make any necessary adjustments to your strategy.

Step 4: Make Improvements Where Necessary

Continuously evaluate your portfolio to identify areas for improvement. Look for opportunities to diversify your investments, minimize fees, and optimize your asset allocation. Keep an eye on market trends and economic indicators that may affect your investment strategy.

Journal Entry: Use your progress journal to identify areas for improvement in your investment strategy. Write down specific action steps you can take to address these areas and improve your overall investment performance.

Step 5: Information Is Power

Always stay informed about developments in the financial markets and how they affect your investment strategies. Read books, attend seminars, and follow reputable financial news sources to deepen your understanding of different kinds of investments. The more you know, the better equipped you'll be to make smart investment decisions.

Journal Entry: Keep a list of recommended books, websites, and other resources that you can refer to for financial knowledge. Record key takeaways from seminars, webinars, or workshops you attend. Regularly review and update your knowledge base to enhance your understanding of investing principles and strategies.

Step 6: Adapt to Evolving Financial Goals and Market Conditions

Be flexible and adaptable in your approach to investing. As your financial goals evolve and market conditions change, be prepared to adjust your investment strategy accordingly. This could mean rebalancing your portfolio, reallocating assets, or exploring other investment opportunities.

Journal Entry: Note down changes in your financial goals and market conditions. Write down any adjustments you make to your portfolio allocation, investment selections, or risk management tactics. Reflect on lessons learned from past experiences and incorporate them into your decision-making process.

Step 7: Adjusting Your Strategy

Once you've identified areas for improvement and adjusted your investment strategy, implement the necessary changes. Regularly review and reassess your investment strategy to ensure it remains aligned with your objectives and prevailing market conditions. This is how you make smart investments earlier in life and build a solid financial foundation for the future.

Journal Entry: Execute the action steps you identified for improving your investment strategy. Track the outcomes of your decisions and evaluate their impact on your overall financial progress. Continuously update your progress journal with new information and insights to maintain a clear record of your progress.

CONCLUSION

So, there you have it.

You stand on the brink of a remarkable journey, one where every step forward brings you closer to reclaiming control over your financial destiny. As you reflect on the insights we've shared throughout this book, remember that you hold within you the power to rewrite your financial story. For a long time, women have been disenfranchised on financial matters, but we're putting that behind us. This book isn't just about teaching you how to approach financial investments, it's also about a reminder of the power of choice. Today, you choose to be a smart investor, so your future self will forever thank you.

We always talk about empowering women to voice their concerns, their stories, and experiences. In the same context, there's no better way to empower women than to empower you financially. A financially secure woman is a powerful force, a transformative phenomenon that can achieve anything she puts her mind to. This is who you are.

Once again, I'll encourage you to put aside any preconceived ideas and misconceptions you might have heard about money. Forget about the societal norms and ill beliefs that hold you back. Think about money as a resource. After all, that's what it truly is. The thing about a resource is that it can only be as effective to you as the use to which you put it.

Some of us come from families or communities where we were made to believe that money is the root of all evil. That's rubbish. In some communities, you are discouraged from talking about money—discard those thoughts. Money is like your car. Treat it well, service it regularly, and it will serve you diligently. On the other hand, if you misuse it, you might pay the ultimate price. Regular service and maintenance for your money means looking for growth opportunities, learning how to save your money, and in a broad sense, making it work for you.

As we wrap up our lovely discourse, I'll reiterate the three teachable moments I'd want you to take from this. First, there's the vision of investing wisely. It is a journey that begins with understanding your financial goals and risk tolerance. By identifying what you want to achieve through investing and how much risk you're comfortable with, you can tailor your investment strategy to suit your needs. This might involve setting specific goals, such as saving for retirement, buying a home, or funding your children's education, and then determining the appropriate investment vehicles to help you reach those goals.

An avid investor understands that this requires discipline and patience. Markets may fluctuate, and there will inevitably be ups and downs along the way. However, when you're focused on your long-term goals and adhere to your investment plan, you can weather the storm and ultimately reap the rewards of your patience and perseverance. Remember, successful investing is not about timing the market or chasing short-term gains, it's about staying the course and trusting in the power of compounding returns to grow your wealth over time.

If you're going to invest, you must have some money set aside, hence the need for diligent savings, our second teachable moment. Saving is the cornerstone of financial independence, providing the financial cushion you need in the face of unexpected expenses, pursuing your goals, and building wealth for the future. To save effectively, you must learn how to work within a budget that outlines your income, expenses, and savings goals. Be honest with yourself about your spending habits and identify areas where you can cut back or eliminate unnecessary expenses. By living below your means and prioritizing saving, you can ensure that you're consistently putting money aside for your future.

If you don't already have one, I'd also encourage you to consider setting up an emergency fund to cover unexpected expenses. Aim for at least three to six months' worth of living expenses to provide a proper financial safety net. Once again, saving also calls for discipline and staying focused on your long-term goals. Avoid the temptation to dip into your savings for non-essential purchases, and instead, remind yourself of the bigger picture and the financial freedom that awaits you.

Our third teachable moment is the need for financial literacy. This is something I realized that a lot of women struggle with. Knowledge is power. Knowledge of financial literacy is about more than just understanding the basics of budgeting and saving. It is more about a comprehensive understanding of how money works and how to make it work for you. You'll need to learn about fundamental financial concepts, for example, compound interest, inflation, risk management, and asset allocation, because these factors directly influence your money's ability to work for you.

Financial literacy also means developing good financial habits and behaviors. This includes setting clear financial goals, creating a budget and sticking to it, living within your means, avoiding debt whenever possible, and regularly reviewing your financial progress to ensure you're on track to meet your goals. The world of personal finance is constantly evolving, with new products, regulations, and economic trends emerging all the time. Be curious, ask questions, and seek out opportunities to continue learning and growing.

Our holy trinity of financial literacy, diligent savings, and your approach to investment are key to defining your future success. If you can cultivate these habits, you can build a strong financial foundation that will serve you well throughout your life.

Moving on, I encourage you to remember that achieving financial independence is not a destination, but a lifelong journey. Stay committed to the principles outlined in this book, and with dedication, perseverance, and a willingness to learn, there's no limit to what you can achieve.

Go forth with confidence, knowing that you possess the tools, knowledge, and mindset to create the financial future you desire. Your journey towards financial independence starts now. Embrace it, own it, and watch your dreams become your reality.

Glossary

401(k): A tax-advantaged retirement savings plan sponsored by employers that allows you to contribute a portion of your salary to individual investment accounts, often with your employer matching contributions and potential tax benefits.

Annuity: A financial product typically offered by insurance companies that provides a series of periodic payments to the annuitant (the person who holds the annuity) in exchange for a lump-sum investment or a series of contributions.

Asset: Any resource with economic value that an individual, corporation, or country owns or controls with the expectation that it will provide future benefits.

Asset Allocation: The strategic distribution of investment funds across various asset classes such as stocks, bonds, real estate, and cash equivalents to optimize risk and return.

Asset Management: The professional management of investments on behalf of individuals, institutions, or entities to achieve specific financial objectives, such as capital appreciation, income generation, or risk mitigation.

Bear Market: A market condition characterized by declining asset prices, investor pessimism, and widespread selling, typically defined as a sustained decline of 20% or more from recent highs.

Bull Market: A market condition characterized by rising asset prices, investor optimism, and widespread buying, typically defined as a sustained increase of 20% or more from recent lows.

Bond: A debt investment where you loan money to an entity (usually a corporation or government) that borrows the funds for a defined period at a fixed or variable interest rate.

Capital Gain: The profit realized from the sale of a capital asset where the selling price exceeds the purchase price.

Capital Preservation: The strategy of protecting the value of an investment portfolio by minimizing the risk of loss, usually prioritized by conservative investors or those nearing retirement.

Compound Interest: Interest calculated on the initial principal and also on the accumulated interest from previous periods, resulting in the exponential growth of an investment over time.

Cryptocurrency: Digital or virtual currency that uses cryptography for security and operates independently of a central authority, utilizing decentralized control through blockchain technology.

Derivative: A financial contract whose value is derived from the performance of an underlying asset, index, or entity.

Diversification: The practice of spreading investments across different assets or asset classes to reduce risk exposure.

Dividend: A portion of a company's earnings distributed to shareholders as a reward for their investment in the company's stock.

Equity: Ownership interest in a corporation, entitling the holder to a portion of the corporation's assets and profits.

Exchange: A marketplace where securities, commodities, derivatives, and other financial instruments are traded, facilitating the buying and selling of assets between buyers and sellers.

Exchange-Traded Fund (ETF): A type of investment fund traded on stock exchanges, holding assets like stocks, commodities, or bonds and offering diversified exposure to a particular market or sector.

Financial Advisor: A licensed professional who provides personalized financial advice and guidance to clients, assisting them in managing their investments, retirement planning, tax strategies, estate planning, and other financial matters.

Financial Independence: The state of having sufficient personal wealth to live comfortably without the need to actively work for basic necessities.

Hedge Fund: An investment fund that pools capital from accredited investors or institutional investors and employs various strategies to generate high returns or mitigate risk, often with higher fees and less regulatory oversight compared to traditional investment vehicles.

Index Fund: A type of mutual fund or exchange-traded fund (ETF) that seeks to replicate the performance of a specific market index, such as the S&P 500 or the Dow Jones Industrial Average, by holding all or a representative sample of the securities in the index.

Inflation: The rate at which the general level of prices for goods and services rises over time, eroding purchasing power and reducing the real value of money.

Investment Portfolio: A collection of assets such as stocks, bonds, real estate, and cash equivalents held by an individual or institution to meet financial goals.

Leverage: The use of borrowed funds or financial instruments to increase the potential return on investment, magnifying both gains and losses.

Liquidity: The ease with which an asset can be converted into cash without significantly impacting its market price.

Liquidity Risk: The risk that an investment cannot be easily converted into cash without significantly impacting its market price, potentially leading to losses or difficulties in meeting financial obligations.

Market Capitalization: The total value of a company's outstanding shares of stock, calculated by multiplying the share price by the total number of outstanding shares.

Mutual Fund: A professionally managed investment fund that pools money from multiple investors to purchase a diversified portfolio of securities, offering investors access to a wider range of investments with lower individual risk.

Passive Income: Income earned from sources other than employment, typically generated from investments in real estate, stocks, bonds, or other financial instruments.

Risk Management: The process of identifying, assessing, and prioritizing risks followed by coordinated efforts to minimize, monitor, and control the probability and impact of adverse events.

Risk Tolerance: Your ability and willingness to endure fluctuations in the value of your investments or to accept the potential loss of capital in pursuit of higher returns.

Robo-Advisor: A digital platform or software program that provides automated, algorithm-driven financial planning and investment management services with minimal human intervention.

Securities: Financial instruments representing ownership (equities) or debt (bonds) in a publicly-traded company, government, or other entity, traded on financial markets.

Stock: A type of security representing ownership in a corporation, entitling the holder to a proportionate share of its assets and earnings.

Wealth Management: A professional service involving financial planning, investment management, and other advisory services aimed at preserving and growing wealth for individuals and families.

Yield: The income generated by an investment, typically expressed as a percentage of the investment's cost or market value, calculated by dividing the annual income (such as interest, dividends, or rental income) by the investment's price or face value.

REFERENCES

Adamczyk, A. (2019, September 4). *This is when people start saving for retirement—and when they actually should.* CNBC; CNBC. https://www.cnbc.com/2019/09/04/the-age-when-americans-start-saving-for-retirement.html

Alouani, N. (2020, February 4). *How to (Re)Program Yourself to Alter your Default Reactions.* Medium; Mind&Stuff. https://medium.com/mindandstuff/how-to-re-program-your-default-reactions-m-s-7877fb462061

Amadeo, K. (2022, March 30). *Pros and Cons of Investing in Stocks.* The Balance. https://www.thebalancemoney.com/stock-investing-for-the-individual-investor-3306182

Awoye, J. (2022, February 2). *Op-ed: The good, the bad and the ugly when it comes to non-fungible tokens.* CNBC; CNBC. https://www.cnbc.com/2022/02/02/here-are-the-pros-and-cons-when-it-comes-to-non-fungible-tokens.html

Backman, M. (2020, July 9). *Don't rely on Social Security alone for your retirement. Here are 3 reasons why.* USA TODAY; The Motley Fool. https://www.usatoday.com/story/money/2020/07/09/3-reasons-rely-social-security-alone-retirement/112065854/

Baldridge, R. (2024, March 28). What Is Your Investing Time Horizon? *Forbes.* https://www.forbes.com/advisor/investing/investing-time-horizon/

Baldwin, A. (2022, June 21). *Hardware wallet vs software wallet: What's Better? | Cryptopolitan.* Cryptopolitan. https://www.cryptopolitan.com/hardware-wallet-vs-software-wallet-crypto-wallet-choices/

Bautis Financial. (2021, May 17). *Bautis Financial.* Bautisfinancial.com. https://bautisfinancial.com/the-power-of-investing-young/

bdhSterling. (2023, June 21). *6 important factors that could determine the income you'll need in retirement.* BdhSterling. https://bdhsterling.com/6-important-factors-that-could-determine-the-income-youll-need-in-retirement/

Bomidwar, K. (2023, May 23). *The Modern Way of Investing Money and the Future of Financing.* Times of India Blog. https://timesofindia.indiatimes.com/readersblog/the-indian-shastrarth/the-modern-way-of-investing-money-and-the-future-of-financing-54176/

Boughton, N. (2022, June 29). *Eight key factors that affect cryptocurrency value.* Wealthprofessional.ca; Wealth Professional. https://www.wealthprofessional.ca/news/industry-news/eight-key-factors-that-affect-cryptocurrency-value/367834

Brian Tracy. (2011, December 19). *5 Reasons Why Most Don't Become Wealthy.* Brian Tracy. https://www.briantracy.com/blog/general/5-reasons-why-most-dont-become-wealthy/

Brotman, E. (2021, July 19). Retirement Panic Is Starting Early: Why Adults In Their 20s Are Already Worried About Retirement. *Forbes.* https://www.forbes.com/sites/ericbrotman/2021/07/19/retirement-panic-is-starting-early-why-adults-in-their-20s-are-already-worried-about-retirement/?sh=3fbb4837bc6c

Bylund, A. (2022). *What Are Risks of Trading Cryptocurrencies | The Motley Fool.* The Motley Fool. https://www.fool.com/investing/stock-market/market-sectors/financials/cryptocurrency-stocks/risks-of-cryptocurrency/

Campbell, B. (2019, October 24). *Why do teens need to care about retirement? | SecureFutures.* SecureFutures. https://securefutures.org/why-do-teens-need-to-care-about-retirement/

Caplinger, D. (2020). *How to Invest in Bonds: A Complete Guide | The Motley Fool.* The Motley Fool. https://www.fool.com/investing/how-to-invest/bonds/

Chandler, S. (2022, November 21). *Proof of Stake Vs. Proof of Work: What's the Difference?* Business Insider; Insider. https://www.businessinsider.com/personal-finance/proof-of-stake-vs-proof-of-work?r=US&IR=T

Chen, J. (2023, May 25). *Risk: What It Means in Investing, How to Measure and Manage It.* Investopedia. https://www.investopedia.com/terms/r/risk.asp

Chen, J. (2024, January 29). *What Is the Stock Market, What Does It Do, and How Does It Work?* Investopedia. https://www.investopedia.com/terms/s/stockmarket.asp

Clark, M. (2021, March 3). *NFTs, explained: what they are and why they're suddenly worth millions.* The Verge; The Verge. https://www.theverge.com/22310188/nft-explainer-what-is-blockchain-crypto-art-faq

CliffsNotes. (2015). *Quiz: Compound Interest.* Cliffsnotes.com. https://www.cliffsnotes.com/study-guides/algebra/algebra-ii/word-problems/quiz-compound-interest

Cointelegraph. (2023). *The NFT marketplace: How to buy and sell nonfungible tokens.* Cointelegraph; Cointelegraph. https://cointelegraph.com/learn/the-nft-marketplace-how-to-buy-and-sell-nonfungible-tokens

Consumer Financial Protection Bureau. (2023, October 19). *How does compound interest work? | Consumer Financial Protection Bureau.* Consumer Financial Protection Bureau. https://www.consumerfinance.gov/ask-cfpb/how-does-compound-interest-work-en-1683/

Conti, R., & Schmidt, J. (2024, January 10). What Is An NFT? How Do NFTs Work? *Forbes.* https://www.forbes.com/advisor/in/investing/cryptocurrency/what-is-an-nft-how-do-nfts-work/

Cooks-Campbell, A. (2022, July 11). *The Importance of Knowing Yourself: Your Key to Fulfillment.* Betterup.com. https://www.betterup.com/blog/the-importance-of-knowing-yourself

Copeland, T. (2023, September 11). *What is the difference between Bitcoin and Ethereum?* The Block; The Block. https://www.theblock.co/learn/249537/what-is-the-difference-between-bitcoin-and-ethereum

Corporate Finance Institute. (2023, January 17). *Robo-Advisors.* Corporate Finance Institute; Corporate Finance Institute. https://corporatefinanceinstitute.com/resources/wealth-management/robo-advisors/

Costa, M. (2023, October 20). *Rich VS Wealthy: 3 Key Differences Between The Two.* Clever Girl Finance. https://www.clevergirlfinance.com/rich-vs-wealthy/

Crypto.com. (2023). *What Influences the Price of Crypto?* Crypto.com. https://crypto.com/university/crypto-price

Crypto News. (2022, June 14). *Pros and Cons of NFTs: Everything You Need to Know.* Crypto News. https://cryptonews.com/news/pros-cons-of-nfts-everything-you-need-know.htm

Curry, B. (2023, December 11). What Is A Stock Split? Why Do Companies Split Their Stock? *Forbes.* https://www.forbes.com/advisor/investing/what-is-a-stock-split/

Daly, L. (2021). *How to Store Cryptocurrency | The Motley Fool.* The Motley Fool. https://www.fool.com/investing/stock-market/market-sectors/financials/cryptocurrency-stocks/how-to-store-cryptocurrency/

Das, A. (2023, June 25). *How technology is reshaping investment landscape.* Deccan Herald. https://www.deccanherald.com/business/how-technology-is-reshaping-investment-landscape-1231167.html

Davis, C., & Taube, S. (2019, July 25). *How To Invest in Stocks.* NerdWallet. https://www.nerdwallet.com/article/investing/how-to-invest-in-stocks

Deenanath, V., Danes, S. M., & Jang, J. (2019). Purposive and Unintentional Family Financial Socialization, Subjective Financial Knowledge, and Financial Behavior of High School Students. *Journal of Financial Counseling and Planning, 30*(1), 83–96. https://doi.org/10.1891/1052-3073.30.1.83

DeNicola, L. (2023, October 8). *The Pros and Cons of Buying Bonds.* Experian.com; Experian. https://www.experian.com/blogs/ask-experian/pros-cons-of-buying-bonds/

Divecha, D. (2017, November 30). *Developmental Science.* Developmental Science. https://www.developmentalscience.com/blog/2017/11/29/teenagers-might-have-a-problem-with-respect-but-its-not-the-one-you-think

Duggan, W., & Powell, F. (2023, August 15). *Top 10 cryptocurrencies of 2024.* USA TODAY Blueprint; USA Today Blueprint. https://www.usatoday.com/money/blueprint/investing/cryptocurrency/top-10-cryptocurrencies/

Dunn, E. (2023, May 23). *38 ways to invest in yourself and build a better future.* Intuit Credit Karma. https://www.creditkarma.com/income/i/invest-in-yourself

Earth Justice. (2023, October 11). *The Environmental Impacts of Cryptomining.* Earthjustice. https://earthjustice.org/feature/cryptocurrency-mining-environmental-impacts

Ezenwa, C. (2017, May). *3 REASONS WHY INVESTING IN YOURSELF IS YOUR BEST INVESTMENT DECISION.* WealthyGen, Inc. https://wealthygen.org/investing-in-yourself/

Farley, A. (2022, September 28). *Why Should I Consider Investing?* Investopedia. https://www.investopedia.com/ask/answers/why-should-i-invest/

Fernando, J. (2024, February 28). *The Power of Compound Interest: Calculations and Examples.* Investopedia. https://www.investopedia.com/terms/c/compoundinterest.asp

Fidelity. (2023). *Should I invest in crypto? | Benefits and risks of cryptocurrency | Fidelity.* Fidelity.com. https://www.fidelity.com/learning-center/trading-investing/crypto/risks-and-benefits-of-crypto

FIKAA. (2023, April 25). *The future of investing: How technology is changing the way we select our investments!* Linkedin.com. https://www.linkedin.com/pulse/future-investing-how-technology-changing-way-we-select-our/

Fischer, K. (2023, May 1). *TikTok May Undermine Trust in Science Among Teens and Young Adults | REBOOT FOUNDATION.* REBOOT FOUNDATION | Promoting and Developing Critical Thinking Tools and Resources. https://reboot-foundation.org/tiktok-may-undermine-trust-in-science-among-teens-and-young-adults/

Folger, J. (2023, July 30). *Investing vs. Trading: What's the Difference?* Investopedia. https://www.investopedia.com/ask/answers/12/difference-investing-trading.asp

Fonville, M. (2020, February 2). *9 Reasons Why Retirement Planning is Important.* Covenant Wealth; Covenant Wealth. https://www.covenantwealthadvisors.com/post/9-reasons-why-retirement-planning-is-important

Frazier, L. (2024, February 20). Why Teenagers Should Start Investing Early...And 3 Proven Investment Tips For Any Age. *Forbes.* https://www.forbes.com/sites/lizfrazierpeck/2023/02/01/why-teenagers-should-start-investing-earlyand-3-proven-investment-tips-for-any-age/?sh=6f29736670e0

Garnett, A. G. (2023, November 16). *Pros and Cons of Investing in NFTs.* Investopedia. https://www.investopedia.com/pros-and-cons-of-investing-in-nfts-5220290

Gillis, A. S. (2023). *risk appetite.* Security; TechTarget. https://www.techtarget.com/searchsecurity/definition/What-is-risk-appetite

Grossman, A. (2024, March 14). *About Money Prodigy.* Money Prodigy. https://www.moneyprodigy.com/teenage-goal-setting-worksheets-pdfs/

Haag, J., & Resnick, B. (2021, October 20). *How to Take Control of Your Bond Portfolio's Interest-Rate Risk.* AllianceBernstein. https://www.alliancebernstein.com/corporate/en/insights/investment-insights/how-to-take-control-of-your-bond-portfolios-interest-rate-risk.html

Hall, J. (2021). *What Is Fiat Currency? Definition and Examples | The Motley Fool.* The Motley Fool. https://www.fool.com/terms/f/fiat-currency/

Hall, M. (2023, December 31). *7 Steps to a Successful Investment Journey.* Investopedia. https://www.investopedia.com/investing/steps-successful-investment-journey/

Hamilton, D. (2023, June 4). *Ethereum vs. Bitcoin Mining : Why They Are Different.* CoinCentral. https://coincentral.com/ethereum-mining-vs-bitcoin-mining-which-is-more-profitable/

Hayes, A. (2023, September 5). *What Type of Brokerage Account Is Right for You?* Investopedia. https://www.investopedia.com/investing/types-brokerage-accounts/

Hayes, A. (2023, December 15). *Blockchain Facts: What Is It, How It Works, and How It Can Be Used.* Investopedia. https://www.investopedia.com/terms/b/blockchain.asp

Hayes, A. (2024, February 20). *10 Important Cryptocurrencies Other Than Bitcoin.* Investopedia. https://www.investopedia.com/tech/most-important-cryptocurrencies-other-than-bitcoin/

Hicks, C., & Powell, F. (2023, February 17). *What is a brokerage account?* USA TODAY Blueprint; USA Today Blueprint. https://www.usatoday.com/money/blueprint/investing/what-is-a-brokerage-account/

Hussar, A. D. (2012, June 26). *6 Reasons Why You're Not Too Young to Get Ready for Retirement Now.* SELF; SELF. https://www.self.com/story/6-reasons-why-youre-not-too-yo

Iacurci, G. (2023, June 7). *Crypto is Gen Z's most common investment. That may be risky, experts said.* CNBC; CNBC. https://www.cnbc.com/2023/06/07/crypto-is-gen-zs-most-common-investment-that-may-be-risky.html

IRS. (2016). *Types of Retirement Plans | Internal Revenue Service.* Irs.gov. https://www.irs.gov/retirement-plans/plan-sponsor/types-of-retirement-plans

Jean-Pierre, T. (2022, February 26). *Why Investing In Yourself Is Always the Best Investment | Curious.* Medium; Curious. https://medium.com/curious/why-investing-in-yourself-is-always-the-best-investment-68f26601e709

Joshi, A. (2024, March 21). Why Is the Crypto Market Rising Today? *Forbes.* https://www.forbes.com/advisor/in/investing/cryptocurrency/why-is-crypto-going-up/

Joury, A. (2022, October 4). *Proof of Stake Versus Proof of Work: Understanding the Differences.* Built In. https://builtin.com/blockchain/proof-of-stake-versus-proof-of-work

Kagan, J. (2024, February 28). *Insurance: Definition, How It Works, and Main Types of Policies* . Investopedia. https://www.investopedia.com/terms/i/insurance.asp

Khuramshahnawaz. (2023, July 26). *The Impact of Technology on Personal Finance and Banking.* Medium; Medium. https://medium.com/@khuramshahnawaz/the-impact-of-technology-on-personal-finance-and-banking-43e7b2eeecff

Klimashousky, D. (2023, August 24). *Making an Investment Plan: A Step-by-Step Guide - SmartAsset | SmartAsset.* Smartasset.com. https://smartasset.com/investing/how-to-make-an-investment-plan

Kobliner, B. (2018, May 7). Why Boys Are Getting More Money Talk Than Girls. *Forbes.* https://www.forbes.com/sites/forbes-summit-talks/2018/05/07/why-boys-are-getting-more-money-talk-than-girls/?sh=5f916f6d4185

Lai, C.-P. (2019). Personality Traits and Stock Investment of Individuals. *Sustainability (Basel)*, *11*(19), 5474–5474. https://doi.org/10.3390/su11195474

Ligon, M. (2024, February 20). Council Post: How Artificial Intelligence Is Revolutionizing Stock Investing. *Forbes.* https://www.forbes.com/sites/forbesbusinesscouncil/2023/07/17/how-artificial-intelligence-is-revolutionizing-stock-investing/?sh=7af002436485

Lin, N. (2023, September 6). *Most Teens Interested in Investing, Few Have Started, Fidelity Reports | PLANADVISER.* PLANADVISER. https://www.planadviser.com/teens-interested-investing-started-fidelity-reports/

Lockert, M., & Tarpley, L. G. (2023, December 26). *How to Invest In Stocks: A Step-by-Step Guide for Beginners.* Business Insider; Insider. https://www.businessinsider.com/personal-finance/how-to-invest-in-stocks?r=US&IR=T

Louisiana Federal Credit Union. (2024). *How men and women spend their money differently.* Louisianafcu.org. https://www.louisianafcu.org/articles/how-men-and-women-spend-their-money-differently

Majbour, B. (2023, February 15). Council Post: How Technology Is Transforming The Investment Landscape. *Forbes.* https://www.forbes.com/sites/forbesbusinesscouncil/2023/02/14/how-technology-is-transforming-the-investment-landscape/?sh=3deb64fe12e4

Maranjian, S. (2019, March 20). *20 Common Beginner Investor Mistakes -- and How to Avoid Them.* The Motley Fool; The Motley Fool. https://www.fool.com/retirement/beginner-investor-mistakes-how-to-avoid.aspx

Matthews, K. L. (2022, September 28). *A beginner's guide to investing in the stock market.* Fortune Recommends; Fortune. https://fortune.com/recommends/investing/how-to-start-investing/

Mband, T. (2022, April 11). *Why Most People Never Get Rich.* Linkedin.com. https://www.linkedin.com/pulse/14-reasons-why-most-people-never-get-rich-titus-mband/

Mitchell, C. (2022, March 17). *4 Factors That Shape Market Trends.* Investopedia. https://www.investopedia.com/articles/trading/09/what-factors-create-trends.asp

Moreano, G. (2023, March 2). *7 best ways to invest in yourself.* Bankrate Press; Bankrate.com. https://www.bankrate.com/investing/best-ways-to-invest-in-yourself/

Muthukumar, K. (2021, June 21). *Five common investing biases that can hurt your portfolio.* Scripbox. https://scripbox.com/blog/five-common-investing-biases-that-can-hurt-your-portfolio/

Napoletano, E. (2023, September 13). How To Invest With Dollar Cost Averaging. *Forbes.* https://www.forbes.com/advisor/au/investing/dollar-cost-averaging/

Napoletano, E., & Schmidt, J. (2024, March 28). Active Vs Passive Investing: What's The Difference? *Forbes.* https://www.forbes.com/advisor/investing/passive-investing-vs-active-investing/

Ndzomga, F. (2023, February 27). *Investing for Beginners: A Step-by-Step Guide to Building Your Investment Portfolio*. Medium; Money and Time. https://medium.com/money-and-time/investing-for-beginners-a-step-by-step-guide-to-building-your-investment-portfolio-b1b774b69516

O'Shea, A. (2019, April 5). *What Are Stocks and How Do They Work?* NerdWallet. https://www.nerdwallet.com/article/investing/what-are-stocks-how-they-work

Orem, T., & Sham, J. (2018, December 5). *5 Steps to Retirement Planning in 2024: An Introduction & How-to Guide*. NerdWallet. https://www.nerdwallet.com/article/investing/retirement-planning-an-introduction

Oury Clark. (2022). *How to set investment goals*. Ouryclark.com. https://www.ouryclark.com/wealth-management/wealth-management-resources/how-to-set-investment-goals.html

People's Credit Union. (2023, October 3). *6 Factors Affecting How Much Money You'll Need in Retirement - People's Credit Union*. People's Credit Union. https://www.peoplescu.com/financial-wellness/6-factors-affecting-how-much-money-youll-need-in-retirement/

Pew Research Center. (2020, September 10). *1. Religious affiliation among American adolescents*. Pew Research Center's Religion & Public Life Project. https://www.pewresearch.org/religion/2020/09/10/religious-affiliation-among-american-adolescents/

Pino, I. (2022, October 7). *How much should you be investing? Some experts recommend at least 15% of your income*. Fortune Recommends; Fortune. https://fortune.com/recommends/investing/how-much-of-your-income-should-go-toward-investing/

Probasco, J. (2024, February 13). *How Much Do I Need to Save to Retire?* Investopedia. https://www.investopedia.com/retirement/how-much-you-should-have-saved-age/

Prosper Marketplace. (2023, June 19). *How to Do a Financial Checkup*. Prosper. https://www.prosper.com/blog/how-to-give-yourself-a-financial-checkup

Pru Life UK. (2024). *How to manage stock market investment risks - Pru Life UK.* Prulifeuk.com.ph. https://www.prulifeuk.com.ph/en/explore-pulse/health-financial-wellness/how-to-manage-your-risks-when-investing-in-the-stock-market/

Public Mutual. (2022). *Understanding the Factors that Influence Bond Prices.* Publicmutual.com.my. https://www.publicmutual.com.my/Menu/Learning-Hub/Understanding-the-Factors-that-Influence-Bond-Prices

Raje, A. (2024, March 13). *What is Investment Insurance?* Kotak Life; ImageObject. https://www.kotaklife.com/insurance-guide/about-life-insurance/what-is-investment-insurance

Reiff, N. (2023, December 31). *What's the Environmental Impact of Cryptocurrency?* Investopedia. https://www.investopedia.com/tech/whats-environmental-impact-cryptocurrency/

Rivetto, L. (2019, May 21). *Teens have the most valuable component to accumulating wealth.* 4-H Youth Money Management. https://www.canr.msu.edu/news/teens_have_the_most_valuable_component_to_accumulating_wealth

Rose, S. (2023, October 9). *Financial Goals Worksheet to Rock Your Money.* OppLoans; OppLoans. https://www.opploans.com/oppu/financial-literacy/financial-goals-worksheet/

Rossolillo, N. (2021). *How to Buy and Sell NFTs | The Motley Fool.* The Motley Fool. https://www.fool.com/investing/stock-market/market-sectors/financials/non-fungible-tokens/how-to-buy-nft/

Royal, J. (2017, September 29). *Active vs. Passive Investing: Which is Better?* NerdWallet. https://www.nerdwallet.com/article/investing/active-vs-passive-investing

Royal, J. (2024, March 20). *12 most popular types of cryptocurrency.* Bankrate Press; Bankrate.com. https://www.bankrate.com/investing/types-of-cryptocurrency/

Rudeloff, M. (2019). *Does gender matter for the use of learning opportunities? Potential explanation for the gender gap in financial literacy - Michelle Rudeloff, Taiga Brahm, Marina Pumptow, 2019*. Citizenship, Social and Economics Education. https://journals.sagepub.com/doi/full/10.1177/2047173419892208

Salvucci, J. (2022, November 29). *What Is a Fiat Currency? Definition, Function & Characteristics*. TheStreet; TheStreet. https://www.thestreet.com/dictionary/fiat-currency

Santander, B. (2024). *Tipos de fondos de inversión*. Banco Santander; Banco Santander. https://www.bancosantander.es/en/faqs/particulares/ahorro-inversion/tipos-fondos-inversion

Schwab Brokerage. (2017, February 2). *What Is Dollar Cost Averaging?* Schwab Brokerage. https://www.schwab.com/learn/story/what-is-dollar-cost-averaging

Shadforth. (2021, November 19). *Cryptocurrency - investment or speculation? - Shadforth - Plan today to live a more confident tomorrow*. Shadforth - Plan Today to Live a More Confident Tomorrow. https://www.sfg.com.au/insights/shadforth_blog/investment-vs-speculation

Sharma, R. (2024, March 17). *Nasdaq Composite vs. S&P 500 vs. Dow: What's the Difference?* Investopedia. https://www.investopedia.com/nasdaq-vs-sp500-vs-dow-5213252

Singh, S., & Jain, A. (2023, March 22). How Does Insurance Work As An Investment? *Forbes*. https://www.forbes.com/advisor/in/insurance/how-to-make-money-using-insurance-as-an-investment/

Sleight, M. (2024, February 16). *How to Find the Best Life Insurance Policy for a Teenager*. MoneyGeek.com; MoneyGeek.com. https://www.moneygeek.com/insurance/life/best-for-teenagers/

Smith, L. (2022, June 21). *5 Insurance Policies Everyone Should Have*. Investopedia. https://www.investopedia.com/insurance/insurance-policies-everyone-should-have/

Sourcescrub. (2024). *Blog: Investment Banking Technology Trends for 2024 | Sourcescrub*. Sourcescrub.com. https://www.sourcescrub.com/post/2024-trends-investment-banking

Sovbetov, Y. (2018, February 17). *Factors Influencing Cryptocurrency Prices: Evidence from Bitcoin, Ethereum, Dash, Litcoin, and Monero*. Ssrn.com. https://papers.ssrn.com/sol3/papers.cfm?abstract_id=3125347

Spector, N. (2023, June 8). *I'm a Retirement Planner: Here's Why You Shouldn't Rely on Social Security Benefits*. Yahoo Finance; Yahoo Finance. https://finance.yahoo.com/news/m-retirement-planner-why-shouldn-170009285.html?guccounter=1

Stanford Online. (2022, June 30). *How does blockchain work?* Stanford Online; Stanford University. https://online.stanford.edu/how-does-blockchain-work

Syben, R. (2022). *Coping with the unpredictability of financial markets - Investment Collective*. Investment Collective. https://investmentcollective.com.au/coping-with-the-unpredictability-of-financial-markets/

Tardi, C. (2021, October 9). *Decentralized Market Definition*. Investopedia. https://www.investopedia.com/terms/d/decentralizedmarket.asp

The Ticker Tape. (2023, June 22). *The Power of Patience and the Four Stages of Stock Cycles - Ticker Tape*. The Ticker Tape. https://tickertape.tdameritrade.com/trading/four-stages-stock-market-cycle-16049

Thrivent. (2023, February 7). *A Simple Guide to the Many Types of Retirement Accounts | Thrivent*. Thrivent.com; Thrivent.com. https://www.thrivent.com/insights/retirement-planning/a-simple-guide-to-the-many-types-of-retirement-accounts

Topa, G., Lunceford, G., & Boyatzis, R. E. (2018). Financial Planning for Retirement: A Psychosocial Perspective. *Frontiers in Psychology, 8*. https://doi.org/10.3389/fpsyg.2017.02338

Tretina, K., & Schmidt, J. (2024, March 11). How To Buy Cryptocurrency. *Forbes.* https://www.forbes.com/uk/advisor/investing/cryptocurrency/how-to-buy-cryptocurrency/

University of York. (2022, March 21). *Artificial intelligence and its impact on everyday life - University of York*. University of York. https://online.york.ac.uk/artificial-intelligence-and-its-impact-on-everyday-life/

Vaidhyanathan, J., & Jain, A. (2024, January 10). What Is Cryptocurrency And How Does It Work? *Forbes.* https://www.forbes.com/advisor/in/investing/cryptocurrency/what-is-cryptocurrency-and-how-does-it-work/

Vasudeva, S. (2023). Cryptocurrency as an investment or speculation: a bibliometric review study | Emerald Insight. *Business Analyst Journal, 44*(1), 34–50. https://doi.org/10.1108//BAJ

Versace, C., & Abssy, M. (2022, September 23). *How Millennials and Gen Z Are Driving Growth Behind ESG*. Nasdaq.com. https://www.nasdaq.com/articles/how-millennials-and-gen-z-are-driving-growth-behind-esg

Voigt, K. (2020, July 15). *What Is a Fund?* NerdWallet. https://www.nerdwallet.com/article/investing/fund

Voigt, K., & Benson, A. (2017, June 15). *What Are Bonds and How Do They Work?* NerdWallet. https://www.nerdwallet.com/article/investing/what-is-a-bond

WalkMe. (2023, August 7). *WalkMe Blog*. WalkMe Blog. https://www.walkme.com/blog/digital-technology-investments/

Weiss, B. (2022, January 28). *Complete guide to retirement planning for any age | Facet*. Facet. https://facet.com/retirement-planning/the-complete-guide-to-retirement-planning/

Windgate Wealth Management. (2015, July 15). *The Power of Compound Interest and Why It Pays to Start Saving Now - Windgate Wealth Management*. Windgate Wealth Management. https://windgatewealth.com/the-power-of-compound-interest-and-why-it-pays-to-start-saving-now/